UNTOLD STORIES OF MISSIONARY YOO

UNTOLD STORIES OF MISSIONARY YOO

ByungKook Yoo

WEC PUBLICATIONS

Copyright © ByungKook Yoo 2009

ISBN 978-0-900828-87-4
10 9 8 7 6 5 4 3 2 1

First published 2010 by WEC Publications
Bulstrode, Gerrards Cross, Bucks, SL9 8SZ, England

British Library Cataloguing in Publication data.
A catalogue record for this book is available from the British Library.

WEC PUBLICATIONS

CONTENTS

CONTENTS

FOREWORD

The Yoo family! What special people – not just colleagues in our international WEC mission family, but also friends for over 25 years. It is a privilege for me to introduce them to you. So much have their lives been entwined in ours that when Jill, my late wife, wrote her book for children in 1990, *You Can Change the World*, her section on Korea majored on telling the story of their two older MK children, Jean and Lam!

Korea! You need a little background information about this remarkable nation to understand some of the moving, often humorous and sometimes sad stories of their years of service in West Africa. Korea is a small, mountainous country with few natural resources and surrounded by large, often bullying, nations – China to the west, Japan to the east and Siberian Russia to the north. Koreans have had to be iron-willed fighters to gain and retain their independence – a fact that has made them so successful in our globalizing world – in industry, generation of wealth, education and above all spiritually with a massive Christian Church with a strong vision for outreach. Koreans are determined goal-getters who will not give up easily.

The twentieth century for Korea was both traumatic and remarkable. It was traumatic – first because of the Japanese invasion of 1910 and subsequent 35-year occupation until the end of World War II. Then, on the USSR dictator Stalin's insistence, the suffering land was divided in 1945 into what became the Communist North and the non-Communist South. In 1949 the North invaded the South with Russian and then Chinese help. The 3-year Korean War left the country devastated, the people traumatized and impoverished, cities and industry destroyed and its beautiful mountains denuded of forest. Who could have thought that within a generation South Korea would host the Olympic Games (1988) and become one of the world's leading industrial nations with a first-world standard of living?

Korea is also remarkable for its response to the Gospel of the Lord Jesus Christ. Only a little over 100 years ago there was not a single Protestant Church in the country, but through some remarkable mission work – especially by the Presbyterians, a strong Church was established that from its early days was self-upporting, self-governing and self-propagating. Today nearly a third of the population claims to be Christian, and of the 10 largest Christian congregations in the world 8 or 9 are in Seoul, the capital city of South Korea. God gave a series of prayer-centred revivals, the last major one being during and after the Korean War. In the mid-70s there were about 30 or so Korean missionaries serving in other lands, but by 2005 that number had grown beyond 12,000, with Korea now the second largest foreign missionary-sending country on earth after the USA, and far surpassed the numbers sent out by the UK. The Korean Church is vital and visionary, but it also has its problems – which have contributed to slower growth or even stagnation in the 21st Century. Past successes can lull missionaries into thinking they have the answer to the world's needs, but unwittingly this can be an export of a Korean Christian culture rather than the more transferable biblical basics. Hence some of the lessons learnt in Africa which are shared in this book!

God led the Yoos to WEC, a pioneer church-planting mission serving in some of the most challenging countries on earth. We were then very much a western mission, but realizing that we had to become more multi-cultural and global. The communication skills and humour of ByungKook and BoIn have helped us to become more international, and, since leaving Africa, their unusual gift in recruiting people has further pushed us in this direction. Koreans now comprise the second largest of the 50+ nationalities that make up WEC in 2006. That, in itself, has its challenges for culture, leadership style, goal setting, expectations on the field, decision-making, etc.

Their missionary service was in Africa – in an area where the great majority of the population and its many peoples is Muslim, which meant that for any missionary agency to operate, there had to be a ministry of practical help to the country. WEC started as a field concentrating on medical work, but was not so well equipped to plant churches. The Yoos with their church life and experience came to the field with the vision of church planting, and found ways of making this happen. They were instrumental in seeing a viable family of indigenous churches emerge. This helps to explain why they needed to work as they did.

You will find ByungKook writing with passion, and exposing his human-ness! Missionaries are not perfect, and God is still working on us all to form us in the image of Christ. This is not a book on how to be a good missionary, but there are many important lessons for us to learn which are packaged in real-life situations and people.

May this book be both a pleasurable and challenging read!

Patrick Johnstone
WEC International
Author, *Operation World*

PREFACE

I was born in Cheong-Song, a small, poor village in one of the most rural regions of Korea. Among the village families, predominantly followers of Confucian ideas, my mother was the first person to become a Christian. As my father, who severely disapproved of her new faith, watched my mother walk miles to church every Sunday, he grew extremely hostile and continuously tormented her. I had a closer relationship with my mother than with my siblings and spent the most time with her. At ten years of age, I began to attend my mother's church. I was my mother's first spiritual fruit and the second in my family to be saved.

What began with a 10-year-old's first trip to church grew into a relationship and then a steady walk with God. The pivotal point of my walk with Christ came in my high school years. As there was no high school in our village, I had to leave my home and go to a large city to further my education. There, I discovered who Christ is on a whole new level and became actively involved in a church that became my family. As we grew together in the Lord, I could not get the image of my own father throwing my mother's Bible across the room out of my mind. That is when I decided to devote my life to God and become a fulltime minister for Him. I hoped if I became a pastor, perhaps my whole family would come to know Christ.

With this motivation, I studied at a Christian university with the goal of attending seminary. In the middle of my university course, I was required to go through three years of mandatory military training. My life remained quite ordinary until I returned to finish university. Then I received the vision for going into missions abroad. At that time, in the mid 1970s, the idea of overseas missions was still very new and unknown territory for Koreans. The number of missionaries from Korea serving in foreign countries was less than ten.

This incredible vision of spreading the gospel to people of foreign lands changed my life. I encountered opposition and disapproval when I spoke of my new life direction. Most people did not understand why I wanted to travel far away and risk so much when there were still many unbelievers right at home. My parents particularly had a difficult time taking in my decision. However, nothing was going to stop me. My heart was thrilled and consumed with the idea.

Perhaps different from other people, I decided to get married solely for the purpose of having a partner in missions. I met a young woman running an evening school for disadvantaged youth who were unable to attend school during the day because they had to work. Certain she would be an incredible help to me on the field, I decided she was the one. Surprisingly, she took a liking to this underweight and awkward country fellow with hair as straight as razor blades, and willingly accepted the marriage proposal of this mission-crazed man.

Soon after marriage to BoIn, I began attending seminary. By the time I graduated, I had become the father of two little daughters. Time was passing by quickly and yet moving abroad was not as simple as I had thought. After making extensive building renovations, my home church fell into debt and asked if I could wait while they repaid most of the debt so they could better support me. Feeling the urgency of my call, I decided instead to take a leap of faith and leave anyway, having neither a church nor even an individual promising to support my family. Keeping my eyes desperately fixed on Jesus, I uprooted my family, left all I knew behind, and headed to England for missions training.

With our 3- and 2-year-old daughters in our arms, my wife and I began our new lives with mixed feelings of anxiety and eagerness as we waited to see what the Lord had laid out for us. The three years spent learning English and taking missionary training courses were a time of countless trials that challenged us emotionally, physically, and spiritually, and drove us deeper into God's embrace and love.

In this country so foreign to us, we knew no one and felt no sense of home. Barely able to communicate our basic needs, we felt utterly lost. As God pulled us through each and every hardship we encountered, we continued to be astounded by His endless grace. He never left our sides through language learning, Missionary Orientation Course, and all necessary training. He was our solace, our nourishment, our peace, the fulfiller of all our needs: good and faithful Jesus.

During our training, while we prayed for direction as to our field, God pointed us to the next chapter of our lives: Africa. As we attempted to prepare for our new life, our first lesson was breaking out of our comfortable cultural shell. Being the first long-term Korean missionaries to join WEC, learning to be part of a predominantly Western family of missionaries definitely taught us a thing or two about cultural competence and understanding which humbled and matured us at the same time. Accustomed to my action-and-goal-oriented cultural tendencies, learning to work hand-in-hand with exhaustively thorough step-by-step-minded Western missionaries was a transition as smooth as ... any word on the opposite end of the spectrum from "smooth". Of course, their working with the Korean newcomers from an entirely different culture, whose accents created a new English dialect all its own, made for many interesting and amusing memories. Without those times where we scratched our heads in utter confusion, struggling to make sense of or to clear up a misunderstanding, a significant portion of this book would not have been written!

Contrary to what we expected, after ten years abroad when we grew to love Africa, God pointed us back to Korea, now almost a foreign place to us. Our next calling was to establish a WEC Korea Sending Base. At that point, Korea was a nation densely populated by churches with thriving ministries and teeming with people, a valuable human resource of tremendous potential for missions. Young people, particularly, were growing restless, eager to discover God's will for their futures. The need for workers who could nurture and develop this potential was apparent to us. We felt this conviction placed on our hearts by God, but at the same time, leaving Africa would be painful. There, we were confident of our purpose, our job, and the growth of our ministries. Looking ahead, the thought of starting over again in Korea and working in an area where we felt completely inexperienced seemed daunting and bleak. But God's instruction to us was unequivocally clear.

The transition was far from smooth, especially for my wife who was heartbroken about leaving Africa. Furthermore, many of our supporters did not fully understand why we left a growing ministry in Africa, a place of immense need, and returned to start a mission organization in Korea, where there already were many other mission agencies. Many believed it was too late to start a Korean WEC headquarters which would only be in the shadow of the existing well-established organizations and doubted it would succeed. In the midst of all the uneasiness, we trusted that God was sending us to Korea to fill a specific need and kept our eyes set on him. June 1997 marked the official launch date of the WEC Korea Sending Base.

The launch part went smoothly; the mystery of "what do we do next" perplexed us. We clung to the comfort of knowing everything was in the hands of the One who sent us. If everything had fallen right into place, the journey would not have been interesting enough. Just as we were about to take our first steps as an organization, Korea was rocked by financial crises. The International Monetary Fund stomped around the corner and plunged Korea into a whirlpool of havoc and bankruptcy. Churches all around us were calling their missionaries home as they were unable to support them any longer. We were back at square one. The future of WEC Korea seemed as though it would evaporate. All our angst, however, was met by God's never-ending faithfulness and wisdom, and only through His grace did we manage to continue our Sending Base work.

Now, twelve years of countless trials and joys later, the WEC Korea Sending Base has sent out more than 400 full-time Korean missionaries, all incredibly gifted and capable individuals passionate for God. This far exceeds any outcome I had dreamed of! I am amazed and humbled by the work of God's hands.

What does God have planned for us in the future? He has emblazoned in our hearts the vision for international mobilization. The Master calls out to His servants, "The harvest is plentiful, but the workers are few!" Even with my broken English and a body that at times seems like it's breaking down, I have no choice but to run after the One who has faithfully guided my steps my whole life. He will speak for me when my English fails me, and He will be my bionic legs when I have no strength to walk any further. His grace will always be sufficient for me.

And of course, I have my precious family to keep me going. Bo In, my loving wonder-woman wife who has stood by me, is the wind beneath my wings. My eldest and most sensible daughter Jean, my personal doctor, is completing her residency at Johns Hopkins Medical Institute. Lam, my personal comedian with Chronic Middle-Child Syndrome (as she says), who marches to the beat of her own drum, has dedicated her life to serving people with disabilities. Last but not least, my youngest daughter, one of the main characters in this book, Yevon, is a freshman at university. I have been richly blessed.

ByungKook Yoo

PART I

ALL FOR
THE LORD?

1

MANGO MAYHEM!

Before heading to the mission field, as much as my body mass said otherwise, I was able to eat a decent amount of almost anything. Growing up in the shadow of the Korean War which so devastated my country, my family was so poor I would frequently find myself gnawing on tree bark to appease my hunger. Being picky about food had never been an issue for me. Leaving my home country, I was convinced that if I could eat tree bark and still be happy and alive, then certainly I would be able to adapt to and enjoy food from any country.

However, upon my arrival in Africa, I learned that perhaps I did not know myself as well as I thought. I found I was not too fond of oily foods such as fried egg, fried rice, fried potatoes – basically anything fried. African food forced me to re-analyze my food preferences. The dishes in our area of Africa primarily consisted of rice and a type of sauce with palm oil as its base. A lot of times, the food seemed to be drowning in a thick pool of palm oil lying at the bottom of the bowl. Meal times were a great opportunity for meaningful fellowship with the Africans, so skipping meals was not a real option, nor was eating something else because there really wasn't much else. Unfortunately, no matter how many times I ate the food, successfully digesting it without painful stomach problems seemed to be no more than wishful thinking. The solution was to pretend to eat and enjoy the food while eating as little as possible.

Before going to Africa, I was about 5 kg below the average weight of men my height. After living there for a while, my scrawny body and extremities weighed an unimpressive 53 kilograms (116.6 pounds) or so. Throughout these years of undernourishment came a temporary season of hope: the mango season. Unless one has tasted the local mangos, words cannot describe how incredibly mouth-wateringly delicious these mangos are. When it comes to the mangos picked at peak season, to refer to them as the king of fruits may be doing them an injustice. Although one must take into consideration that perhaps, because I barely had any other choices of fruit, my appreciation for these mangos may have been magnified even more.

Regardless, it is difficult to describe how much I like mangos and I don't see my undying adulation for those particular local mangos dissipating any time soon. During mango season, I felt as though my steps were lighter than air. I was actually able to *enjoy* meal times, during which I would satisfy my insatiable mango appetite with delectable mangos, day in and day out. For breakfast, one large juicy mango in my stomach and I was OK. However, when lunch time come around I would have to eat with my African friends and students. According to their culture, not eating simply because I did not like their food was considered a social taboo. So, as usual, I resorted to eating as little as possible while pretending to eat plenty. Meal times were jolly and pleasant and so was my stomach as it had been amply filled with mangos before the meal.

It is such a shame that the mango season lasts only about two months. Afterwards I went back to ten months of an agonizingly empty stomach. Consequently, I found myself fighting a wave of depression around the time mango season was coming to an end. In hopes of finding even one more mango, I would rummage through all the markets. Eventually, I would end up with a strange collection of leftover mangos that resembled old, greenish-brown prunes. Slight obsession maybe? Perhaps. Nonetheless, despite my unyielding devotion to these mangos, as if they were laughing at this pathetic, starved missionary, they would swiftly disappear, leaving me mango-less and hungry.

One year, as I was about to set aside my temporary mango insanity and face the world again, a fellow missionary (who probably pitied me) brought me the most extraordinary news. In an area along the outskirts of our country, a man from a neighboring land owned a nursery of young mango trees that bore the best of his country's mangos. To my pleasant surprise, he had trees that bore fruit much earlier than the local ones *and* he even had trees that yielded mangos *after* our normal mango season was over. Now this, my friends, was good news. Exceptionally good news!

Stepping back into my world of mango insanity, I bought all the trees in that nursery, triumphantly brought them home, and planted them in all possible square yards of our entire compound. To prevent goats and sheep from eating the young trees, I put up fences around each precious tree. My children complained of having nowhere to play, but it was as if I had new children to pay attention to: my mango trees. Morning and night, watering those trees became more important to me than any other work I had to do. Even my staff members suffered, for on days they forgot to water the trees I found myself getting angry and on some occasions even raising my voice. Without a care in the world, after all the love and devotion they received, the mango trees did not let me down and grew beautifully. Three years passed and they were taller and thicker than a human. Four years passed and they started blooming with flowers, a sign indicating mangos were soon to come. I believe I nearly lost my mind when I saw those flowers and probably got more excited than necessary. I recall barely resisting the urge to run and dance around the trees. There may have been a couple of occasions, when no one was looking, in which I could not resist anymore. As I stared into the blossoms, I imagined all the mangos that would bud from these flowers and anxiously awaited the day when I could slam the door in malnourishment's face. Whenever my children ran around the compound, I feared they would somehow knock off the flowers of those 10-foot tall mango trees. Thankfully, whenever I begged them to *walk* (slowly) and be careful not to hurt the trees, they would comply, shaking their heads as they tip-toed around the trees, probably not out of any concern for the trees but away from their father who had truly lost his mind.

Lo and behold, a few months later all my efforts paid off when the flowers withered and one by one little green mangos appeared. Four years of restless waiting, and these trees once again did not let me down. Welling up with gratefulness, there were days when I would gaze lovingly at the trees, smiling to myself while my wife and children as well as the natives watched nervously from afar. It didn't matter to me what they thought because I knew that in just a few months those mangos would ripen. I would be able to reward my hard work and sink my teeth into juicy mangos as sweet as honey. This feeling was an immense fuel for me, that no one can understand, that enabled me to be more hopeful and livelier than ever.

The mangos continued to grow to the size of a child's fist. Give them two months and they would be ready to eat! The excitement – unimaginable!

2

MISSIONARY IN A SUIT

The insanely hot weather in Africa always made wearing nice clothes incredibly difficult. Actually, it made wearing any clothes painfully difficult for that matter. Wearing as few layers as possible in order to stay even the slightest bit cooler was a daily challenge. The people that lived in the village were poor and wore few pieces of clothing, which made it easier for us to blend in fashion-wise. The hot sun also did its daily job of roasting our skin into a nice, dark leathery hide. Our clothes, skin color, lifestyle, and behavior began to imitate those of the local people. As much as I knew it was ideal to blend in, to be honest with you my vanity began to get the better of me and my reflection in the mirror started to strangely bother me. I had changed so much.

When I first arrived, all eager to be a humble servant for the Lord, I graciously accepted the way things were. The clothes (or lack thereof), food, lifestyle, cultural differences were fine. I was the foreigner so if I was treated like an alien or clumped in with the Chinese laborers who lived here, that was OK, too.

Of course, things changed! The various idiosyncrasies I had previously accepted with a smile became a source of irritation. The differences between the local people's ways of thinking and mine began to bother me, and I frequently found myself arguing with them over petty things. Often frustrated by the things they did not understand, I landed myself in pointless debates that only left me more frustrated. Whatever happened to being a good example spiritually and mentally?

Hundreds of Chinese people lived in this country doing construction work. Unfortunately, they were treated rather poorly by the local people and viewed as an inferior race. They didn't speak English or the local language which left little opportunity for interaction with anyone outside their Chinese community and only perpetuated discord with the local people. Young and old alike took great pleasure in jeering at Chinese people whenever they saw them. From "slanted eyes" and "flat nose" to *"Ching-Chang-Chong"*, the wisecracks and Kung Fu gestures never seemed to die down.

To the local people, we were Chinese. White people were *"tubab"*, which means "white man" and Asian people automatically were labeled as "Chinese". Perhaps it was my Korean pride or fear of being looked down upon welling up within me, but I began to stop whatever I was doing and snap back, "I'm Korean, not Chinese. Get it right!" I would usually get the same response, "Well you have slanted eyes and a flat nose, what difference does it make? Either way you all look funny." I couldn't take it anymore. I simply had no patience left.

"I have my own nationality. If only you knew the great country Korea is, you wouldn't be talking," I would angrily grumble as I walked away.

"Don't let it bother you," my wife would say as I huffed and puffed around but I wasn't hearing anything she was saying. Pacing angrily around my room, I stopped to look at my own reflection in the mirror, suddenly overcome by my own misery. "Look at that, who is that dreadful person looking back at me?" I exclaimed. My face looked aged and tired, my skin was dark and rough, my hair was matted with sweat and dirt. I almost didn't recognize myself anymore.

A few days later I got a call from a close friend in Korea who was planning to visit us. He called me to make last minute confirmations and see what things he could get for my family before he took off. Oh, the list was long. We needed Korean food, books, magazines, toys, videos, summer clothes ... my long lost youth. "A suit for me will be great, thanks," I said.

"A suit? But in that weather, when are you ever –" he started.

"Yes, just a suit," I answered.

There was a short pause but then he agreed and hung up the phone. I could tell he thought I was rather strange but I didn't really care. Soon I would have a nice, fashionable suit to wear and look handsome and sophisticated. I would show them. Said I looked funny, did they? I wanted so much to be able to put on that suit and prove to everyone – but mostly to myself – that I was still a gentleman despite my appearance screaming otherwise. "Besides, the suit might look rather nice with a tanned complexion," I said quietly as I looked at the dark country man staring back at me in the mirror. I needed to reassure myself that, even though my life here had taken a toll on my spirits, my confidence and my appearance, with a little bit of polishing up I could be back to my old self once again. Of course, not one day out of the year here calls for a suit to be worn. Even if it did, it would be drenched with sweat within minutes which is why I had not brought one in the first place.

My friend finally arrived and I can so vividly remember how excited I felt when he handed me the fine Italian-made suit. I snatched it out of his hands and leapt to the next room, squealing like a little girl, to try it on. "This is madness, when will I ever need to wear this?" I thought, but I just didn't care. For the next couple weeks, when I got home after work I would pull out the suit and try it on again. I would stroll over to my children's room pretending to look for something and they would jump around excitedly telling me I looked so smart and handsome. Children are great to have around sometimes.

As ecstatic as my children were, I couldn't help but notice the fact that I looked so, well, ridiculous. Despite the neatly combed hair and freshly washed face, I still looked like a cow farmer who had been plucked right off the field and dressed up with a suit for his first date. Regardless, I was still convinced the local people needed to see me dressed up and looking professional because I wasn't about to be undermined any longer. I would find "coincidental" opportunities for the local people to catch me in my suit. The more I carried on this nonsense, the louder the voice in my head got, "ByungKook. What on earth is going on with you? You are wandering around in a useless suit like an idiot with nowhere to wear it to. Some missionary you are ..."

I couldn't stand it any longer. What was I doing wearing a suit around the house? How many more days was this handsome suit just going to hang there in the closet? My wife was watching me out of the corner of her eye and trying to act like she wasn't concerned. She rolled over on the bed mumbling something to herself and pretended to sleep. It was late. I was tired from working and being vain all day so I lay down next to her to try to get some rest.

"No!" I said as I jumped out of bed and walked over to the closet. I pulled out the suit and started putting it on again.

"Are you serious? Have you lost your mind? If so, where can we find it because this is getting ridiculous, ByungKook!" BoIn exclaimed, looking tired and worried.

I rambled something about how we should go on a date and spend one-on-one time together. She shook her head and rolled over again mumbling with more clarity, "He's crazy." Seeing that asking nicely wasn't going to work, I dragged her out of bed and begged her to go out with me. Obviously irritated, she grudgingly plodded into the bathroom to get ready. I waited eagerly for her in the living room, pacing around in my suit. We would go to the nice hotel in the city where tourists often stayed. They had a fancy little café by the outdoor pool. I thought I'd feel better if my wife and I had a cup of coffee there.

BoIn came out wearing her usual get up, a simple dress that looked like a long T-shirt of tie-dyed material and slippers. She looked like my housekeeper, but I didn't want to make her change. She was already questioning my sanity and I didn't need to fuel her annoyance.

We went to the hotel and sat down in the outdoor café. I tried to look as nonchalant as possible, perhaps like a business man taking a coffee break who was nice enough to invite his housekeeper. The waiter came to take our order. As I ordered a drink, I noticed he kept glancing at me first and then at other people. I turned my head to see what he was looking at and finally began to *see* the people around me. Here I was in my suit while everyone else was in beach wear, half-naked. All eyes were on the strange- looking Asian man in a suit and his giggling housekeeper in slippers. I felt a cold sweat trickling down my back and couldn't get out of there fast enough.

As I rushed back to the car, thoughts tumbled through my mind once again. I had lost my mind! Just lost it! What had come over me? How had I changed so much? This wasn't like me! Whatever happened to being His humble ambassador? Had missionary life sapped me of my sound mind?

My wife was laughing hysterically and couldn't catch her breath as she sat next to me in the car. "Oh, this is too much, I cannot believe how silly you are! Oh my goodness, did you see their faces in there? ByungKook the silly missionary!" Well, at least one of us had enjoyed the evening.

3

AFRICA'S MOST HATED CREATURE

Africa is famous for its swarms of mosquitoes. Swarm is actually too innocent a word. Africa is famous for its invading armies of mosquitoes. I've been told that the number of people killed by diseases caused by these insects is larger than the number of casualties in wars throughout the history of Africa.

For an African, malaria caused by mosquitoes is as common an illness as a cold is in other parts of the world. These insects attack all human beings; male or female, young or old, black or white – all feel the sucking of their blood! The victims are easily stricken. One day the baby next door to us had a fever. By the next morning, he was being buried in the ground. It was frightening to watch. My family was not protected any more than the villagers. We all suffered from malaria. On two different occasions, I was so seriously ill I almost died. During our missionary training for Africa, we had intellectually listened to the lectures about mosquitoes. Yet, when I arrived in Africa and these mosquitoes began to brutally bite my wife and children, I came to abhor them. Before this experience, I would never have dreamed of gnashing my teeth or cursing a creature created by God, but my anger at these insects drove me to it.

Some of my colleagues finally gave up killing mosquitoes. As for me, I could not choose their way. It was a fight for our lives because we had experienced the fatal suffering of loved ones due to malaria in the past. I even considered this battle was Satan's medium for attacking us and turning our focus towards this life or death issue. It was essential that my family take the utmost precautions against the marauding hordes that attacked us day and night.

We had to sleep under mosquito nets all year, causing us to feel suffocated beyond description. Yet we were so psychologically dependent on the increased safety from these nets, that when we were thousands of miles away on furlough we could not fall asleep without the security of a net over us. The mosquito is both evil AND clever. Even with our net precautions the night was a time of feasting for the mosquitoes. If there was even the tiniest hole in the net, the invaders would find it and come inside. Of course, at night it was necessary at times for one of us to move the netting to go to the bathroom. During each exit and entry, the enemies quickly came within our protective screen wall and waited for everybody to sleep again; then the feast began as they gorged themselves on our blood all night long. Sometimes when I awoke in the morning, there would be two hundred bites within just a few square inches on my body. Ohhhh! I would fly in to a rage and shout out, "You evil ones, how dare you bite a skinny man like me?" I found myself calling this out as if those insects were invading soldiers who could hear my cry.

At other times, lying in bed unable to sleep because of the incessant buzzing of the adversary, I would suddenly leap up brandishing my flashlight and try to kill the noisemaker. If I was lucky enough to get it, my temporal quest for revenge would be satisfied, but my quest for sleep would again be disrupted. Occasionally I would find a mosquito that survived my midnight attacks still alive within my borders when I awoke. I was driven to distraction by these creatures, and built up anger and frustration more than I had ever known. When I found one still alive in the morning, I would torture it with vengeance for the bites it gave me during the night. Capturing it in the morning was so much easier than during the night because by morning it was laden with MY blood in its stomach and could not fly away. As before, I spoke to it as if it was human: "You obnoxious, rude, miserable, disagreeable thing. How dare you suck our blood? We have toiled and labored under the hot sun. What have you done? You should never have feasted on us. I'll show you a thing or two."

Of course, I could have crushed the mosquito to death with a piece of tissue, but that would have been far too kind. My hate was so extreme only a slow death would do. I would trap the laden beast under a cup before slowly sending a numbing repellant smoke into that prison cell. Then, after the mosquito had lost its sense of direction, I would leisurely pluck the wings from its measly body and dismember it one leg at a time. At last, following its death, I would experience satisfaction. My wife thought my behavior was irrational. She told me how cruel it was to torture any creature to death. She was right, but with my anger at the mosquitoes and no room for generosity, I didn't know how else to cope. What a pathetic, woeful sight I was standing in triumph by my slain invader. These mosquitoes were the cause of my sleep deprivation and irrational behavior! I hated them not just because of my blood being sucked out, but because of the harmful side effects they produced: lack of sleep, painful diseases, and even death for some people.

Honestly, I could not pray that God would grant me love for the mosquitoes. I was already struggling enough in prayer with my need to love the local people. I was beginning to feel that the mosquito was the one part of God's creation we were permitted to hate. It may seem ridiculous that I was fighting so venomously against mosquitoes, but I was no longer the same person who had arrived in Africa. Whenever I heard mosquitoes flying, I gnashed my teeth. This silly reaction made me look and feel miserable, taking me down to the level of this creature that I judged absolutely useless.

Living in Africa had changed me. I needed help desperately!

4

HAVE I GIVEN UP ALL?

Here in this land of Africa, would there ever be a day when I could eat the things I truly longed to eat? The only fruits and vegetables available were mangos, oranges, onions, and strange weeds posing as herbs. For the basics there was a grocery store closer to the city, run by refugees who had fled from neighboring countries plagued with civil wars.

One food was always on my mind: *kimchi*, a spicy pickled side dish made from Chinese cabbage. Back at home, *kimchi* was in endless supply. Only after I came to Africa did I realize I had taken it for granted. There were days I could imagine the taste of *kimchi*, its attractive smell, its crisp texture, and its unique flavor so clearly. If only I could take a handful of that stimulating goodness and put it in my mouth! I was clearly suffering from *kimchi* withdrawal. Most difficult for me were the times when I lay ill with malaria. Feeling hopeless and miserably appetite-less, I felt as though right at that moment if I could have one bite of *kimchi* I would feel better immediately and leap out of bed.

My children, who had left their home country at a very young age, weren't too sympathetic about my *kimchi* withdrawal but, as always, my wife knew exactly how I felt. If anything, she suffered more. Sometimes, she would say, "You know, when we go home on furlough, I'm going to ask my mom to make my favorite types of *kimchi* and eat all the *kimchi* I want with a hot, fresh bowl of steaming rice. Every day. Every meal." As I watched her talk about *kimchi* with a dazed look on her face, she looked like a starving baby desperate for a taste of milk. One day I came upon her sitting on the floor with her nose in a Korean magazine talking to herself. Surprised by my wife's bizarre behavior, I approached her carefully. Irritated by the interruption she looked up licking her lips and showed me beautiful pictures of colorful *kimchi* dishes. She couldn't tear her eyes away from the pictures as she rambled on about how delicious the *kimchi* looked and what she would do to get some of it right then. I had rightful reason to be worried that she had momentarily gone mad and scolded her about acting so crazy over *kimchi*. She gave me that look wives give when you don't quite know what they're thinking but you know, "I shouldn't have said that." Huffing, she walked away while I quietly wiped the spit that had accumulated in the sides of my mouth without my wife seeing.

After settling down in Africa, we tried growing Chinese cabbages during the cooler months of December and January. We had seeds sent to us from Korea and diligently watered them in our garden. For me, seeing tiny green sprouts come out of the ground despite the intense heat was marvelous. I faithfully nurtured them with prayers in the morning as well as at lunchtime. I believe my prayers for their growth were as eager as my prayers for the spiritual growth of the local youth. Then a frightening and most unexpected thing happened. As soon as the sprouts began breaking through the dirt, the caterpillars came and ate them all up! No matter how hard I tried to kill the creatures, it seemed there was no end to their numbers. They took advantage of the rare succulent greens rising up out of the dry land. Whenever I found these gluttons, I would fly into a rage and brutally kill them all. Besides the persistent attack of these enemies, the green sprouts were drying out under the scorching sun. A feeling of anger surged as I took pity on the dying leaves and patted them. I decided to take real action and made a trip out to the Ministry of Agriculture. When I got home, the caterpillars were still munching away at my defenseless cabbages, not knowing that I had a lethal weapon in hand.

The Ministry of Agriculture had warned me that due to the high toxicity of this pesticide, the cabbages would no longer be fit for human consumption, but the sight of the little beasts munching brought tears of frustration and anger to my eyes. I poured the whole bottle of pesticide on the baby cabbages while saying to the caterpillars "If I can't eat these cabbages, than neither can you." The cabbage leaves disintegrated within thirty minutes. The persistent caterpillars, however, gnawed away at the stems right up to the point of their death. I planted Chinese cabbages again and again, but eventually had to give up. Although I was born and raised in the countryside, I confess I had never done any kind of gardening before.

One day, BoIn came home yelling "I've got some Chinese cabbages!" I saw a sack full of lettuce in her hands.

"What? Did you say Chinese cabbages?" Sure enough, her hands were full of cabbages, "But they're just regular lettuce!" I said. She kept insisting they were Chinese cabbage, and as I stooped down to take a closer look, I realized they really were Chinese cabbages even though they were miniature, about the size of my fist.

The five hundred Chinese people living in this African country at the time had found a way to raise Chinese cabbage. What a wonderful surprise! BoIn and I immediately started making *kimchi* with Korean chili powder and local hot chili peppers.

"Oh, *kimchi*, it has been such a long time since I last saw you!" We attacked the *kimchi* like starving hyenas. We had craved it for such a long time that my whole family ate *kimchi* with bread at breakfast, with rice at lunch and plenty again at supper. I thought I would never suffer from malaria again. At night, BoIn would get out of bed, disappear for a while and slip back in after grabbing a bite of *kimchi*. Some western colleagues who stopped by would comment on the strange smell in the house, but it didn't matter to us. I was glad they didn't know how delicious *kimchi* was, but then I wondered if they longed for a slice of cheese the way we had wanted *kimchi*, and I could empathize with them.

We were no longer anxious about having *kimchi* because a generous Chinese man promised to supply us with Chinese cabbage at any time. My whole family was excited! We no longer minded eating the fluffy long grain local rice because we had *kimchi* to eat with it.

Then, I began having stomach pains. I have had a weak stomach since childhood so I get sick easily. There was no doubt I had more than just an upset stomach. It had been quite some time since I had eaten hot and spicy food, and I had now been consuming *kimchi* in excessive amounts. The pain increased and would not go away even when I skipped meals.

Though I became seriously sick, I could not resist sneaking bites of *kimchi* behind BoIn's back. My stomach continued to get worse and as a result I had to go see a doctor. I was told that my stomach was swollen and seriously impaired and that I needed to stay on a strict diet for one month. Otherwise, I could suffer even more serious problems.

My diet consisted of a bowl of porridge and a piece of dried local bread for each meal. BoIn was so worried about my stomach that she prayed and fasted for me for a whole week. What a lovely and gracious wife! As a result, my family stopped eating *kimchi* for my sake. The Chinese man who supplied us the Chinese cabbages didn't come by anymore as if we had already told him to stop bringing them. The pleasure of eating *kimchi* seemed to have been a part of a dream. It was as if God had decided to pour out His grace on a couple of souls lusting after pictures of *kimchi* in a magazine – if even for a short while. Strangely enough, I began to hate the smell in the gas-fridge left behind by the *kimchi*. How ashamed I was of my weakness and how disappointed I was in myself. Was I not the one who had proudly bragged about going to Africa to sacrifice all I had? Look at me now! Was it so hard that you could not keep a single piece of *kimchi* from your mouth, ByungKook?

5

MY SAVIOR, BOYAK?

I've never been particularly healthy or strong, quite the opposite, and I'm not the only one who always worried about how my health would fare in Africa. Many suggested that I build up my strength and immune system with an oriental herbal medicine, *boyak*, before leaving. One evening, an older deaconess from a church where I had spoken approached me after service, "While you were up there talking about your vision, I couldn't help but notice how weak you looked. How is anyone ever going to take you seriously? I am going to get some *boyak* for you and you must take it." For all I knew, *boyak* was a dark, thick herbal tonic that smelled and tasted horrible so I flatly refused.

As she kept insisting that I start taking *boyak*, I finally gave in and agreed to try it. I did my own research on *boyak* and came to the conclusion that it couldn't hurt. No one bothered my wife BoIn about it too much because though she has a tiny frame, she was physically and mentally stronger than me. My ego would have liked it to be the other way around, but nonetheless I happily accepted the case of *boyak* the deaconess brought me, touched by the fact that she cared so much.

I finished the whole case of *boyak* and went to Africa. Though I had been told about the hot climate and mosquito infestations, nothing could have prepared me for what my family encountered there. The burning heat and swarms of mosquitoes that circled over our heads like crazed vultures were unbearable. The mosquitoes especially targeted BoIn and the children which brought on many sleepless nights of agony. BoIn had a particularly difficult time adjusting to the heat, and dealing with the mosquito attacks on top of that made it all so much worse. The misery is something I still cannot quite find the right words to describe.

I never thought such a tiny creature could be so amazingly powerful. Having your body covered in bites day in and day out truly tries one's sanity to the limits. Just one mosquito carrying malaria can take a person's life. Many nights I would jump about the room swatting away, cursing at the agile pests. BoIn quickly started losing the battle against the mosquitoes that couldn't seem to get enough of her. Malaria, infected bites, lack of sleep, and exhaustion made her weaker each day. She was supposed to be the healthiest one of all of us and yet it wouldn't be an understatement to say that she was sick for most of our first term. No matter how hard I tried, I couldn't divert the mosquitoes away from her and to me instead. They didn't seem to want to have anything to do with me!

Finally, the time for our first furlough arrived. As we looked back on our first term in Africa, I must say we were very grateful for having survived. We came home feeling triumphant, like a general who had just won his first victory. Wherever we went and to everyone we met, we proudly praised God who had so faithfully allowed us to complete our first term successfully. One day we met the deaconess who had given me the *boyak* to take five years before. We started talking about my family's life on the field and the difficulties we had encountered. I began to tell her how strange it was that my wife and children got sick so often but I managed to stay healthy the majority of the time. She was so happy to hear that and said it must be the *boyak* that had kept me strong. I excitedly agreed and rambled on about how great *boyak* must be and how impressed I was with how well it worked. I began to sing a new tune, and the incredible effects of *boyak* soon replaced my acknowledgment of God's grace, which was what really had enabled my family to endure such difficult circumstances.

The time to return to the field quickly approached and I made sure I took a double portion of *boyak*. I also insisted that BoIn take some as well. She really didn't want to but I stubbornly pressed the issue and she reluctantly gave in. *Boyak* made her feel nauseated so she stopped taking it shortly after, which I was not happy about. Soon we headed back to Africa. My spirits were high and I felt confident I wouldn't have to worry about any health problems, especially since I had taken a double dosage of the wonderful *boyak*.

As we expected, the mosquitoes once again tormented BoIn, but I had little sympathy for her this time. "You got yourself into this trouble. This is exactly why I told you to take the *boyak*. Thanks to your stubbornness, now look at what you've gotten yourself into," I grumbled. Later, I felt sorry for being so harsh with her, but my words had already done their damage by adding guilt to her misery.

Three months after settling down for our second term, I found myself lying in bed, dreadfully sick. Completely incapacitated, even moving a finger seemed painfully impossible. My family had been hit with malaria a few times during our first term, but this time it was like I hit a brick wall. My fever was dangerously high, my heart felt as if it couldn't beat any more, and every breath felt like my last. Because we lived in a remote village in the countryside, I knew I could easily die if I didn't get outside help quickly. My health deteriorated and I fell into a state of unconsciousness. Fully aware of the critical situation we were in, BoIn managed to get me into the car and drove for many hours to the nearest hospital. I remember waking up a few times during the drive and looking over at BoIn, clutching the wheel as she drove as if this was the most important trip of her life. I couldn't say anything or even lift my hand to wipe the tears collecting under my neck. My heart ached as I thought about how this could all end and what would happen to my family. Why had I been so blind?

To my shame, I had totally forgotten that God's wonderful grace was what had enabled me to complete our first term despite my weak constitution. I was reminded that only He is in control and always uses the weak to carry out His ministry. I was truly humbled by my own foolishness. How easily my eyes had been turned away from God's grace. I felt like a child who had gotten overly confident in his ability to run and tumbled on to the ground.

I lifted a prayer to the God who had sent me, for what reason I didn't know, to this country to do His work, "Lord, this is the kind of man I am. To others I chattered on about how it was Your grace that sustained us, all the while putting my faith in some foul-tasting tonic. Will you have mercy on this pretentious, hopeless mess of a man?"

Have Thine own way, Lord,
Have Thine own way;

Wounded and weary,
Help me, I pray.
Power, all power,
Surely is Thine;
Touch me and heal me,
Savior Divine.

I didn't know how much time had gone by but I remember waking up in a hospital bed to the sound of this hymn, a recording of a Korean church choir my wife was playing next to my bed. I was still too weak to say anything, but I knew I was going to be all right. I was once again overwhelmed by God's loving grace.

Since then, I have never taken or even touched *boyak* again.

6

THE LEATHER SOFA

I once heard a story that went something like this:

A Korean missionary serving in an Asian country lived in a large, nicely furnished house. One day, the leaders of his sending church informed him they were coming to visit. Knowing what they would think about his luxurious home, he hid half of his furniture in a storage room. Even after he went to all this trouble, the church leaders were disgruntled by the missionary's lavish home and cut off all his support. They felt that the missionary and his family were taking advantage of the financial support they were receiving and putting it into the wrong things.

I have an interesting story of my own when it comes to situations such as this.

The number of stores selling furniture and electronics had been steadily increasing in our part of Africa. Granted, most of them sold second-hand goods, but they were still usable and had a decent amount of life left in them. Most of the furniture and electronics sold here were shipped in from different countries in Europe. The merchants doing business here only payed for the goods to be shipped as they were actually discarded by large stores in Europe. Even though they were considered out-of-fashion or unsellable in the wealthier nations, they were quite valuable in developing countries.

One day as I was walking through the local market, an old sofa caught my eye. Although unattractively faded, I could still see the remnants of a nice brown color. The sofa looked as though it had received a solid beating and was now sitting on the sandy lot collecting dust. No one seemed to want it, so the owner had stuck an extremely cheap price on it hoping he could just get rid of it. I examined the frame which was still quite sturdy, and though the leather looked ugly and discolored, there were hardly any tears in it. I thought about the creaky sponge sofa at home that had begun to smell odd from the sweat from people's bodies. "This couch could actually look quite nice if I just polished and stitched it up a bit," I thought, and I hauled it home that day.

My wife looked completely exasperated by the sight of the sofa. "What on earth did you bring home? Just because it's cheap, it doesn't mean you had to buy a piece of junk like that!" she said. She wasn't the only one who thought me foolish for making such a purchase. The young men hanging around our youth center shook their heads and chuckled as they helped me unload the sofa. Their eyes seemed to say, "Poor man's gone crazy."

I was determined to prove to them, and myself, that I was indeed sane and left to buy black spray paint and shoe wax. I don't remember exactly how much spray paint I used – maybe it was the fumes – but I was very pleased with the end product. Sure, you could see the creases and stitches through the paint but now it was one color and had a great luster and it looked and smelled much better than the sponge sofa. Yes, a nice black tint was left on the rear of those who sat on it the first few weeks, but I'd say that was trivial compared to its plush, leathery comfort. Eventually, everyone was happy with the sofa, even my wife. Fellow missionaries who came to visit all commented on how nice the sofa made the living room look. "What a nice couch, not too fancy, not too shabby. It looks sturdy and very professional!" they would say as they sank into the couch cushions. I felt as though I had discovered a buried treasure.

One day, after a long hard day's work, I was relaxing on the couch and reorganizing my thoughts. We were due for a visit from some supporting church members from Korea. "It'll be nice to see them. We can all sit here and catch up – wait a second!" I sat up quickly. In Korea, only the wealthiest of people like CEOs of huge companies or movie stars could afford leather sofas. You rarely saw a leather couch in a home. What would our visitors say after seeing a leather couch in a missionary's home? It may sound petty, but in Korea, being able to afford the luxury of having leather to sit on meant you had a *lot* of money to spend. What if the visitors thought I was wasting money on frivolous things?

"No, no, come on, this sofa was a piece of junk I picked up and refurbished. This is ridiculous. It's not like I spent a lot of money on it," I muttered, trying to convince myself to stop worrying. It didn't work. "No, this could definitely cause a misunderstanding. You know what Koreans think when they see leather furniture. What am I going to do, explain myself *every* time I think someone's questioning the sofa?" That sounded silly and time consuming. I considered the idea of giving away the sofa, but quickly decided against that. I had put in a good deal of manual labor and sweat under the hot sun to fix up this sofa. "No, this is nonsense! I'm not going to give it away! For what, just because I'm scared of what gossip this might cause? I refuse to let myself be bothered by what others will think! I'm not doing anything wrong! No sir, this leather couch will stay exactly where it is for everyone to see!" I said as I sat up straight and nodded my head.

The next day, I had a sofa cover made.

I bought some thick, non-leather-looking fabric and asked a local man who was good with a sewing machine to make a simple cover. "Now you cannot tell that it is made out of leather and I will not have to answer to anyone!" I said, pleased with what I thought was a brilliant idea. I found myself telling the story to visitors before they even brought up the sofa. It's beyond me why I thought everyone wanted to talk about the couch. "See, it was an ugly old thing, but I fixed it up and made it look really nice – you saw it – anyway, remember, I never bought it brand new. Well, I got a cover put on it because I like to keep things modest," I would go on.

The more I heard myself tell this story, the more pathetic I sounded to myself and I felt the frustration build up inside me. What on earth had happened here and why was I wasting my energy on this? I had bought a raggedy excuse of a sofa, covered it with spray paint and shoe polish, made it look nice, and now I was worried that it looked too nice! A chaotic stream of thoughts tumbled through my mind as I looked at the innocent sofa staring back at me. "Why did I buy this stupid thing anyway? Look at the headache it's causing me! So what if I have a leather couch? It cost less than a shoe! I have nothing to hide! Even if it was expensive, is a missionary allowed to have *nothing* nice?" I said angrily as I tore off the fabric covers and threw them on the floor.

My wife had run out to see what was going on in the living room and was now standing there staring at me with a blank, wide-eyed expression on her face. "What is going on here? Why are you thrashing the covers? If you hated them so much you shouldn't have put them on there!" she said, not having a clue about what was going on in my head.

"I've got to get this rubbish out of here. I am such a fool!" I exclaimed as I kicked the covers away. BoIn stood there speechless as I stormed out the front door.

I flopped down on the grass trying to regain my senses. "I must be going crazy," I thought, shaking my head. No one had even said anything to me. What was I so worried about? I needed to re-evaluate what was going on in my head. Was I focusing so much on how pious or ascetic my missionary life looked because I felt guilty about not doing enough for the Lord? Had I judged the quality of other missionaries' work by their external belongings? Had my life here caused a spiritual drought in my heart so I had lost touch with things that were really important? What does living a simple life really mean? I didn't think it was really about having a leather sofa or not. Why was I focusing so much on petty things and what the church members at home might think?

Hundreds of questions ran through my mind before I finally stood up to go back inside. My wife had put all the covers back on nicely. I chuckled quietly as I was once again reminded of how simple my mind could be sometimes. If you let your mind run with its thoughts uselessly, it'll get you in trouble. I sat down on the couch and began to pray, "Lord, look at me. A missionary's supposed to be someone that others can look up to and learn from. Do you see what a hopeless man I am, so concerned about what others think and obsessed about how I look in their eyes. Well, from now on, I live just as I am. It's all about what You think and You only, Lord."

7

BEAUTIFUL FACE

When I first met BoIn, I knew I had to marry her soon before
someone else whisked her away. To be completely honest with you,
I don't remember too much about our short courtship period or
even the details of my wife's appearance during that time because I
was in such a hurry to say "I do." Much of it seems like it went by so
fast it's almost a blur. Fifteen years later, my wife and I still feel like
we're in our twenties only to be quickly reminded otherwise when
we see our daughters becoming young women.

Now in our forties, we have a long trail of joys and sorrows that
has taught us what it means to deeply, deeply love each other. I am
so thankful for her willingness to come with me to a foreign land,
leaving all her loved ones at home and making all the amazing
sacrifices that she has by being by my side. I cannot be anymore
grateful for the trust that she put in me as her husband.

Instead of all the best of all luxuries I wanted to surround my
precious wife with, we were met with the blistering heat, ravenous
mosquitoes, and miserable poverty everywhere. The scorching heat
was almost blinding. It was here that I first learned what a
wretched nuisance clothes could be. It felt like I couldn't peel off
enough layers to get cool. When I first arrived here, still a very
conservative Korean countryman, it was very embarrassing for me
to see the native women walk around without any clothes above

their waist or even missionary women wearing sleeveless dresses. Before long, I stopped noticing when I realized that eliminating as many pieces of clothing as possible was simply the wise thing to do in order to survive.

I had a very fair complexion to begin with so even with the deepest tan, I was still not *that* dark. My wife, on the other hand, who was naturally darker than most Koreans, looked like she had been thoroughly over-cooked by the sun. She became unrecognizably dark and well, pretty much unrecognizable overall.

On our way home for furlough, we went through Britain and stayed there for a few days. Ashamed by our own appearance, we decided to have a go at fashion and went shopping for some decent clothes. Everything looked completely ridiculous on us so we finally gave up and headed to the airport. "It will be fine, they'll just be so happy to see us," we reassured ourselves. Our close British friend who took us to the airport incessantly insisted that at least my wife should have something nice to wear and bought her a frighteningly expensive outfit from a shop in the airport.

Looking our best, overpriced shoulder pads in all their glory, we stepped out into the lobby of the airport and saw ten of our relatives and close friends eagerly waiting to welcome us. Not one of them recognized us that day. Eyes wide and jaws gaping, their stunned expressions said enough about how much we had changed. Our appearance that day is still the butt of the jokes among our church friends and relatives. It was truly a reality check for them to see how much the environment can completely change one's appearance.

Just when it looked like our original skin color was coming back, we had to return to the field, back where it felt like the end of the earth. Once again, we were back where there was just no need to keep up with any fashion trends. There was one trend that was the latest craze; the way African Americans over in the States wore their hair had captured the young men here but I wasn't too convinced that those hairstyles would suit me.

It wasn't just fashion that has left me behind, the outside world of pop culture had moved on far ahead without me. I had no clue about famous stars, currently popular films, or what the latest hit songs were. There was one Korean song that I remembered well that I learned while I was going to school as a young man in Seoul. Its lyrics resonated within me as they sounded so appropriate for what I was feeling:

Counting the days away from home, over ten years have passed, and see how my youth has withered.

Feeling homesick and so distant from the rest of the world, I would often sit outside and stare at the moon. The same moon that shone over Korea was looking down on me and it made me feel less far away from home. I would flip through old photos and let my mind wander through past memories.

My heart would sink when I would see BoIn look at old pictures of herself and talk about how she couldn't even recognize herself anymore. She would quietly run her fingers over pictures of her face when she was young and smiling with her friends and family in Korea. There were days when she would refuse to look at herself in the mirror and I knew it was because she didn't want to let her emotions get the better of her. I did my best to tell her she looked beautiful and that I loved her youthful vigor but there was no denying that both of us felt the wear and tear of mission work and had the evidence etched on our faces.

One day, I received a videotape of Korean TV programs that some Korean fisherman had left behind. As my wife and I watched the tape together, I watched carefully to see how different the Korean women on the programs were from BoIn. There was one particular show on there called "Housewives Sing" in which Korean women with families competed against each other in singing. When each woman came on the stage, a subtitle would show up displaying their name and age so it allowed accurate comparison. I chuckled with delight when I came to a wonderful realization; despite all the glitz and glamour surrounding these women, they didn't look too different from BoIn after all! Underneath all the make-up and lacy dresses, they looked just as worn out and if anything, far older than my wife!

BoIn thought I was just happy to watch Korean programs but for me, it was something deeper than that. I think it was the first time I could confront my underlying guilt of bringing my wife far away from everything she knew and making her suffer alongside of me. I watched my wife out of the corner of my eyes as she stared into the screen like a little child enraptured by the world inside of the television. I reached for her hand and said, "Why don't you go do something for yourself that'll make you feel beautiful one of these days?" She turned her darkly tanned face and looked at me with quizzical eyes. Honestly, I'm not so sure who I said that for, whether it was for me in hopes of pacifying my own guilt or letting my wife know that I understood that she desired to feel beautiful as a woman.

Though these words are indeed true, it didn't quite seem fitting at that moment to say, "Forget about your outward beauty; as missionaries, all we must be concerned about is pursuing heavenly beauty and not worldly beauty, my dear." I didn't need to repeat something she already knew. I knew that BoIn put her whole heart into building spiritual beauty and strength.

"Try and stay out of the hot sun as much as you can dear," I said to her, "you don't want to damage that beautiful face." She was still so young and beautiful in my eyes; I wanted her to know that.

8

"DIRTY PORK-EATERS"

This country has changed a lot since my family first arrived. During our first term, there was so little of everything except for dirt and blistering heat. It was common to see people standing in long queues to buy rice or waiting overnight at a gas station to get some fuel. Sometimes we couldn't find any gasoline and had to cook our food over a small burner we had for camping. But things have changed and almost anything can be bought though prices are high.

During our first term, the only meat available at the local market was beef that was tough as rubber. To those who couldn't afford even this leathery meat, fishermen offered strange fish caught in the sea nearby.

One day a man came to my house wanting to sell me some pork. As it was impossible to get pork at the marketplace, I was very pleased and bought all of the legs. Compared to Korean pork legs, they weren't very big, but much cheaper than the rubber-like beef at the market. The man was so happy that I bought from him, and told me he would come to my house every Saturday. When we heard this, we were also happy because now we could have easy access to cheap pork. None of us actually liked pork that much, but at least it would be a good source of nutrition in this barren land. We were pleased with the new arrangement, but none of the local men in my house particularly rejoiced with us. I did not notice the stark expression that took over their faces while we got excited over getting pork.

From that time, we enjoyed all kinds of pork dishes. We invited some of the local fellows for lunch and fellowship and made a flavorful sauce using the pork meat to pour over rice. We all sat down together to enjoy this new dish. As usual, we all gathered around a large bowl and began to eat. The ten of us were eating together when one of them commented, "It's really delicious today! This sauce is so good and the meat is really tender too!" I told them it was pork and proudly proclaimed how much cheaper it was than beef so we could enjoy this more often.

Suddenly, an awkward silence fell and everyone stopped eating. I asked them why they weren't eating, to which they all responded, "I'm full and cannot eat any more." Eyeing all the leftover rice in the bowl, I thought that was really strange since we had just started eating 10 minutes before. Judging by their response to my comments about the pork, I knew something was wrong. Later, a young man named Rame who helped my wife and me in our language study explained the situation. I had completely forgotten that Muslims do not eat pork! They regard pigs as dirty animals and don't even touch them, let alone eat them. I had made an insensitive mistake and completely forgotten about this aspect of their culture. Normally, when foreigners invite locals over for dinner, the guests politely inquire about the meat to be sure it isn't pork. Why they did not ask me, I'm not sure. Perhaps they assumed I would know better, which obviously was too much credit given to me on their part.

The common notion of Christians the locals have is that Christians are religious drunkards who drink alcohol and eat dirty pork. This is based on the story that a group of well-known people here who claimed to be Catholic Christians were reputed to spend all their time drinking strong liquor made from palm juice and getting terribly drunk. Many of them apparently also raised pigs in their homes and ate them. I do not know who these people were, but they had exposed this aspect of their lifestyle enough to give the locals the impression that Christians are filthy drunks. Some local youth have even told me that is the reason they don't want to become Christians; they don't want to be associated with the drunk, pork-eating Christians. Of course, this is unfortunate as it is an unfair representation of Catholics, and is definitely not the reputation of Christians we, as missionaries, want to have working against us.

Inadvertently, I had not only disregarded these men and their religion but I had fitted myself nicely into their image of pork-eating Christians. I didn't necessarily feel I had to stop eating pork because their religion forbids it, but at the same time I did not want to seem disrespectful by indulging in something they saw as so distasteful. I felt I had lost credibility in their eyes, as they were thinking, "Oh, you're one of them." I wasn't sure how to balance it all. How was I to show them that eating pork didn't make me a drunk, and that not all Christians behaved like the ones they had heard about?

I thought hard about what I should do as far as pork was concerned. I was disappointed our eating pork had to become an issue as it was a food my family enjoyed eating. Nevertheless, my wife and I decided we would not eat pork for now and told the pork salesman not to come anymore. He was upset about the loss of business, but he knew there would be other foreigners who would buy pork from him. Both he and our family would manage just fine.

9

A HOUSE TO CALL MY OWN

As soon as I graduated from university, I dove right into three years of seminary and immediately after completing seminary, I started my life as a missionary. I never got to experience working in a company nor did I ever collect a single salary. I did, however, work as a youth pastor in my home church during my seminary years. Through the church I received some funds which were barely enough to cover the cost of my tuition and book fees. Life for my wife and me was a constant financial struggle – perhaps financial battle is a better way to put it. When I was a student at university, as my wife and I passed by, neighbors would whisper, "Oh, there goes that poor college student and his poor little wife. Well, they're still young. Things will start looking up for them once he graduates and finds a good job." Once I started seminary, they now told each other, "Yes, that's the poor seminary student and his poor little wife. But you wait, things will definitely be looking up once he starts a big church and has many followers." Once they found out that I had become a missionary, their final opinion was, "Ah, there goes that poor missionary and his poor little wife. Well, things will start looking up for them once they reach heaven."

Living costs were indeed far beyond our humble budget so settling comfortably in a nice home was out of the question. In fact, living out of suitcases became our way of life because we had to pick up and move so frequently. Rent costs always went up and having to move to another place that was more affordable became almost a regular routine. When other sad memories fade one incident I remember is the time I had barely made a deal with a 20-story apartment owner who agreed to let us move in with him and share his apartment. Two weeks after we moved in, he decided that living with two little girls in the house was not going to work for him after all. I vividly remember that day, in the pouring rain, moving all our soaked belongings out of the apartment, wiping away the heavy rain and tears from my face. As I hauled the luggage that I had just moved in two weeks earlier, I silently wept, praying that my wife would not see.

I knew that this was all part of the sacrifice I had to make from the moment I decided to devote my life to God. I knew that this would be only one out of the thousands of hardships I would encounter as a missionary. These tears were not sorrowful tears of self-pity but, rather, they were a reflection of my even more steadfast dedication to Him.

As soon as I graduated from seminary, I moved my young family to England to begin missionary training. When I left Korea, my home, my family, and friends – that to me had been my real and final move. That day when I packed my bags and left everything I had known my whole life, one more move or a hundred more moves didn't make a difference any more.

Indeed, picking up and relocating my family once again became our lifestyle during our first few years in England. Unable to appease the constant demands and complaints of our first landlord, we moved into the small home of a British friend, a fellow pastor. Despite the wonderful hospitality, after a while we knew our stay was too long and moved to a one-room unit. That room was our kitchen, living room, and bedroom in which my wife, my two young daughters and I all shared one double bed. As my daughters grew, this became more and more uncomfortable. After more unsuccessful moves, we finally came to live in Bulstrode, WEC's British and International Headquarters. Inside Bulstrode, we continued to change rooms. In this vast land, we did not have one home to call our own where we could put our hearts at rest knowing that tomorrow this place would still be ours.

Then, we left England and headed off to Africa to start our new life. When we first moved there, land was exceptionally cheap. To us, this made up for the fact that the weather was unimaginably hot. Because of the inexpensive cost of living, we were able to stay in a much nicer home than we had ever expected. Even with our limited budget, we were able to manage our rent every month – not easily, but we managed without having to fall into debt. Even better, a little while after we moved to Africa, the government of that country began to allow foreigners to buy land. We jumped at the opportunity and with the help of a mission-minded deacon of a church in Korea, we purchased a plot of land for an unbelievably cheap price, in a small village in the middle of nowhere. In Korea, to buy a plot of land that size would be outrageously expensive and simply out of the question for us. It wasn't a huge area of land, but it was big enough for our family to use however we wanted. That was truly a wonderful feeling. Once we had the land we needed to build a house we could live in.

The excitement of being able to start building my own home felt wonderful beyond description. The only difficulty was I had never built a house in my whole life. As a matter or fact, I had never seen a house being built. No, I hadn't even been remotely close to an area where a house was being built. Still, deciding on how many rooms, where the kitchen would be, how many bathrooms we would need, I thought we could definitely do that. I remember one evening my family and I sat on the floor huddled around an old calendar, using the backside to draw a blueprint on. The pure joy we felt taking turns drawing our rooms and creating the design for our own house – I don't think any of us will forget that night, especially my second daughter Lam, who would not stop insisting that we build a house on top of a tree like the movie *Swiss Family Robinson*.

The size of our house was decided. We figured an area of 15 meters by 15 meters would be ample space for the family. To make sure, we outlined the perimeter of our house with string. Standing in the space, it didn't seem that large. If anything, I was worried it might be a bit small, but I thought, "I'm a missionary, what do I need a big house for? Heading to this country, I thought we'd be living in a mud hut." A room for my wife and me, one for my children, an office, a living room, a kitchen, and a guest room for other missionaries: this was enough space for it all. So it was settled and construction began. A fellow missionary and good friend from New Zealand agreed to supervise the construction and very soon we saw the walls of our future house rise. However, to our great surprise, once the walls were about waist high, we began to notice two shocking things. First, for whatever reason, something went wrong, and rather than being rectangular the rooms began to look diamond-shaped. The parallelogram rooms didn't bother us too much, just made our house unique. The other problem was the size of our house. Beyond what any of us had imagined, our 15 meter by 15 meter house turned out to be huge!

The house was nearly finished and there was nothing we could do. If we had spent a bit more time analyzing and carefully watching the construction workers, this could have all been avoided. Tearing down the house and rebuilding was not an option and I grew more and more worried. Why was the house of a poor missionary so big? My feelings about my new house now were not of excitement, but mind-racking stress. I now had this house that in my opinion was too huge for a missionary. What was I going to say when visitors from my supporting churches in Korea saw my house? A great friend of mine from Korea, a fellow pastor, visited us while we were still building the house. As he silently stared at the house with his jaw slightly open, I wondered what he was thinking. The day he left, he pulled me aside and said quietly, "You know ByungKook, it's probably best that you don't show the Korean churches pictures of your new house. They may be tempted to think...bad thoughts about you." Why was I such a fool? I didn't know the first thing about architecture and here was the product of my ignorance. For others, a large house like that may have been a dream come true. To me, however, living in a mud hut like my African neighbors would have given more peace of mind.

We moved into our new house and my children spent the first few hours exclaiming, "Our house is big!" thoroughly entertained by the echo of their voices. We had thought that making our roof very high would be a smart way to keep the house cool. Obviously we overestimated. Again. My wife and I spent the first few hours praying. "Lord," we asked, "while we live in this house, please do not bring any visitors from Korea." The following months, regardless of our feelings, the Lord brought more visitors from Korea to us than we thought possible. *Not* to our surprise, the first remark they made upon entrance into our house was, "Oh my! What a big house!" Rambling on about how we somehow unknowingly built this large house seemed ridiculous so all I could ever do was stand there, unable to reverse this terrible mistake I had made.

Our final solution to somewhat alleviate this situation was to not embellish the house whatsoever. Unable to allow my wife's exceptional flair for decorating, I only permitted a few shelves, a table, chairs, beds, and the bare necessities. When BoIn suggested that since we had a house, we might as well make it look like a nice home instead of a correctional institution, I wouldn't budge, even though I really wanted to agree. "I know, perhaps we should install bars in the children's doors and keep them as our prisoners," my wife would say sarcastically. That did give me an idea. Perhaps we could use the large space in this house for more than just a house. Preferably not for a correctional institution, but something. First, we decided that the largest room in the house would be used as an office and classroom. Then, we decided to make the living room into the Sunday service sanctuary. Now that we had a service hall, we turned the other rooms into Bible study classrooms.

Thankfully, our next door neighbor informed us that he was going to sell his plot of land. It was much smaller and more expensive than the land we already owned, but my wife and I had already made up our minds. We agreed to buy our neighbor's land and rebuild our house: this time it would be small and humble. Even though it meant a lot more outgoing money, we decided it was well worthwhile. We did not want to skew people's notions of missionary life and mislead others about our own beliefs as missionaries. Most of all, we would have peace of mind, not being distracted by an unnecessarily big house, and could focus on the work we were there to do. This time, we built a small, cozy house no one would consider big. Our previous house was turned into a Bible school, and we were all satisfied with the end results of our new home, particularly the rooms which were now definitely rectangular. My wife, especially, was very excited to finally have her own house that she could decorate however she wanted. With that excitement, whenever she had a single free moment she would plant grass in our yard. Where she got the grass, I had no idea. Over the years, I had learned to be quiet and observe. She planted beautiful wild flowers and fruit vines that made our small front yard as beautiful as the Hanging Gardens of Babylon (or at least that's what I told her to stop her from making the backyard into a tropical haven for the mosquitoes). In the areas that were absolutely dry and infertile, my brilliant wife picked up boulders and all kinds of cactus from somewhere and created a small Sahara Desert.

Now, we were not stressed about our home, which came as a huge relief. I don't believe people should have their own house as their source of stress. We could have as many visitors as we wished and not have stress about anything but their comfort. Our yards were filled with all kinds of colorful flowers. Even though I'm not into flowers as much as my wife, I was still overjoyed that I finally had a house where the number of flowers was the only thing I actually had to worry about. I found myself getting excited about the flowers my wife planted because I knew I would be able to watch them grow in *my* yard over the next few years in *my* house.

When we came out to the mission field, we were prepared to live in a mud hut or even a tree house with monkeys as neighbors, which would actually have been a wish come true for Lam. Yet, the Lord gave us a beautiful home with no one around telling us to move out. This was truly a great blessing from God and we were beyond grateful and simply ecstatic. Nothing other than God's love lasts forever and the length of time we were able to live in this dream house of ours was a little less than a year. We had to leave our little house and go Korea to start a new WEC Sending Base there. When we left, however, we were convinced we were going to return to our house, so we left everything the way it was. Every cup, bowl, table, and even our sweat-stained bed was left in place. Now, I wonder, will we ever get to go back to Africa? Will we really be able to spend the rest of our lives with our dear friends there? I'm afraid the outlook, as of now, is not good.

Like I always say, such is the life of a missionary. Someone builds a house, another lives in it. Paul plants the seeds and Apollos follows, watering and nurturing them. We built the house and, hopefully, another missionary will be able enjoy the comfort of the house in the future. Anyway, everything is only temporary in this life and no home is permanent. I'm more excited about the home we will have in heaven, which will *definitely* be permanent. I am ecstatic at the thought!

10

THE BATTLE OF
THE FLOWERS

BoIn, my lovely wife, absolutely loves flowers. To say she absolutely loves them doesn't even encapsulate exactly how much she adores flowers or any living shrub for that matter.

When we first got married, like any other couple we had our fair share of arguments. As much as I would like to say they were graceful disagreements that ended in embrace and love songs, I cannot. They were more like heated, temper-driven fights that sometimes led to four days of cold silence. Quietly seething but also regretting the things we had said without thinking, we didn't yet have the maturity to reconcile with each other by prayer and the Word of God.

One day, however, I discovered an incredibly simple solution to reconciling with BoIn. As a typical Korean countryman, my talent is *not* being able to express myself, but rather stumbling all over an awkward apology that sounds like nonsense in the end. I must say my new-found solution was like a magic trick that saved me after an argument. The best part was that it didn't require any eloquence on my part, just a bundle of beautiful flowers! After an argument, a bouquet of flowers would take away the darkened frown and bring back the color in BoIn's face, and even a smile. How easily this worked! Had it been me, maybe the first time would have worked, but I mean really – they're flowers. BoIn isn't like me though; she forgave me unconditionally as long as I gave her flowers. I was dreadfully poor as a seminary student and I felt guilty for not being able to buy her nice things and the best of foods. But she didn't care. I would pick wild flowers and put them around the house, and that was all my wonderful wife needed.

Sometimes, however, my wonderful wife would go to the grocery store and come back with flowers instead of food! Too poor to understand, I would complain, "If you really loved flowers, you would just let them be. Why are you encouraging the killing of flowers by buying cut flowers? Doesn't this obsession with flowers seem a bit selfish to you?" Of course, then came a fight. Then came flowers. Then came peace.

BoIn took her love for flowers all the way to Africa. Of course, if I had been incredibly fortunate there would have been an endless abundance of captivatingly exotic flowers and my wife would never have had time for anger. But the scorching heat makes survival a constant test for the limited variety of flowers there. Even the trees appear to be suffocating at times while the wild grass always looks freshly powdered with dust. Fortunately my wife was content with the wild flowers (the technical term being weeds) I plucked on my way home. Unlike her, I am completely unaffected by flowers, much less weeds.

The first village we settled in was like a desert with only a few orange trees scattered amongst dry shrubs and dirt. Even after our building construction, the place looked dreadful. The dorm rooms, study room, classroom, and chapel looked as if they didn't want to be there. BoIn suggested we plant grass in the courtyard to block the sandy wind that stung our feet. I was opposed to her idea because of our insufficient water supply.

One day, BoIn discovered a resilient breed of grass called "Bahama" that can thrive in blistering heat without too much water. I stood there watching her squatting on the ground as she planted the seeds one by one and grumbled about how she was wasting her energy over such a useless thing. She ignored me and continued to plant the grass. Over the next few weeks, the grass began to grow despite the dry ground and boiling sun, and the next thing we knew we had a courtyard full of beautiful green grass that was truly a refreshment to our souls.

Ready to move on, BoIn began to plant flowers and plants around the compound. She and I both knew how well the grass turned out so I couldn't argue and just sat by and watched. Sure enough, beautiful roses grew in one corner of the courtyard while a variety of cacti grew in another. Other colorful flowers lined the pathways and curious vines climbed the walls. She raised them with all her heart and gave them much love. The flowers seemed to be encouraged by her devotion and grew strong even under the intense heat. BoIn suffered greatly from the scorching weather and nothing seemed to make her feel better than spending her free time around the beautiful flowers and plants.

Everyone who saw our center couldn't stop talking about how pretty it looked, like a fairyland with the beautiful colors and plush green grass everywhere. Missionaries who visited us would gaze at the roses and talk about how much they missed home, and were so delighted when we gave them some roses to take with them.

Motivated by the joy the flowers brought everyone, BoIn started planting them wherever she went. My wife is incredibly artistically talented. She conjures up beautiful visions in her mind and makes them come to life without any training in decorating or design. With her own hands, she made the place look exquisite.

Almost like a children's fairytale, BoIn walked by and flowers popped up where she walked! There were flowers everywhere. I wasn't sure if my center was a youth center or a flower market anymore. The local young people seemed happy with it. Some would walk the footpaths barefoot, enjoying the textures and colors, while others would lie on the grass under the shade to relax.

Eventually, BoIn started to bring the Garden of Eden inside and I found myself waking up to pollen, walking through vines that webbed the corridors, and picking petals off the floor. We began to argue about her getting carried away with the flowers and not considering the diminishing water supply. We were actually fighting about flowers. Of course, this time I was left with no remedy because she had already put flowers all over the place.

BoIn appealed to me for understanding, "We always have the same food, wear the same clothes, and don't have any family members to visit us. Our contacts are always the same. We do the same things every day." She continued, "If you could just change your attitude toward them. Look! This place is so beautiful now! Don't you remember what this land looked like when we first came here? Now we all enjoy being out there, even the local people come here more! And isn't it a good thing that we're showing some of these youngsters, who blame the hot weather for never going out and doing anything, that if they just put in a little effort they too could improve their surroundings and themselves? They saw me out there all the time, they know I didn't have other people come in here and do it for me, they came with me when I went out looking for wild flowers, they saw me work hard for this! Why not set an example while doing something I love?"

Part of me understood what she was saying. BoIn needed this because it was her way of relaxing. This was her way of getting away from the daily struggles we faced. But the problem was the huge difference between the local village homes and ours. I couldn't help but feel a little uneasy about living in such a well-decorated house and thought it could send out the wrong message. Of course, BoIn was right that with a little bit of effort and grunt work, we had completely changed the appearance of this place, and it was helping us feel better emotionally. As missionaries, were we supposed to deprive ourselves of everything beautiful and live miserably? No. Yet, being the typical Korean, I was worried about how this would affect our image. As much as I hate to admit it, face value matters to me. I found myself wondering what people at home would think. If they saw us living a simple life with nothing, they might say, "Look at Missionary Yoo's family living there in that mud hut and walking around half naked in that heat. They are truly living modestly. What a sacrifice they are making!" I knew people at home had their stereotypes all drawn out about what the austere missionary life is supposed to look like. And here my wife had somehow made our home look like the gardens at the tourist hotel in the city!

At this point I decided I would not let myself get sucked into being so concerned about what everyone else *might* think any more.

Coming from a culture that tends to be extremely worried about looks, social image, and saving face, here I was, halfway across the world and still bound by my cultural propensities. "You can take a Korean man out of Korea, but you cannot take Korea out of the man" – isn't that what they say? All I knew without a doubt was that these flowers were a source of comfort for my wife. I would see the peaceful look on her face when she would retreat to her flowers after a long, hard day of work. They made my wife happy and because of that, I found myself loving the flowers, too.

11

OUT OF KOREA

Living on the mission field, it's easy to lose touch with current events and anything to do with the outside world. When we got to the field, this was the case for us. It was as though we were living in our own world, almost completely unaware of what was going on in the wider world around us. Even "breaking news" reached us long after it had broken, and by the time it got to us it was definitely in bits and pieces that didn't always make sense. Going about in our mission "bubble", we grew quite detached from the rest of the world and used to it being that way.

As anyone can imagine, many times I found myself terribly discouraged and depressed. That was when I felt most homesick and wanted so much to visit Korea. I often listened to Korean sermons sent from home. They were such an encouragement to me. Who knew cassette tapes could bring a man such joy! I always struggled trying to communicate in the local languages and English, so to be able to listen and understand every single phoneme, inflection, and intonation without trying was truly sweet. To tell you the truth, even the dullest of sermons that I wouldn't have paid much attention to back home became interesting and occasionally brought tears to my eyes. I remember days when I would lie on my bed reminiscing about memories from Korea and, before I knew it, I became thoroughly depressed.

For hours I would lie there, lost in my thoughts: "What am I doing here? There are so many more capable, brilliant preachers who could come here and set the lost souls ablaze. I can barely get some kindling to catch a flame. Lord, why didn't you send *them* here instead of an incompetent servant like me? They can speak English, they are overflowing with strength, and have so many gifts you lose count – why did you send a feeble man like me to fight such a fierce battle and make my supporters worry all the time?"

At times I would feel terribly inferior to my fellow missionaries and wanted to drop everything and go home. But the honest truth is, even if we did go back to Korea, there was nothing we could really do there. Even if there had been an opportunity for pastoral ministry waiting for us, I wasn't convinced I could run a Korean church either. I realized I had been teaching basic "Christianity 101" for "spiritual babies" for so long I didn't have confidence in myself to be a pastor in Korea where discipleship training and evangelism had reached unprecedented heights of advancement. Everything was moving along without us in Korea. How would we ever catch up? Maybe this far-away country was where I needed to serve for the rest of my life and where I would even be buried.

I was hit with a harsh reality check when we went home for furlough. One afternoon I was sitting in on a pastors' meeting with some friends of mine who were also pastors. They were discussing current issues in the world and in the church. It was all beyond my understanding and I couldn't follow their conversation despite trying my best to participate. At the end of the afternoon, the unspoken message I heard loud and clear was, "You've been living in the middle of nowhere for so long that you couldn't possibly understand what we are talking about here. Don't give yourself a headache by trying to keep up." Attempting to ignore the ache of a crushed ego, I sat there silently feeling more like an inferior nuisance than an equal among my friends and colleagues.

"God, it looks like there is no place for me here even if I were to leave the ministry in Africa. Korea isn't my home any more. This isn't the same place I used to know and these people are not the people I used to know."

Whether I liked it or not, Africa was now my home. I was told that some single missionaries who went home after serving on fields for over thirty years didn't last long before sadly returning to the field. At home, their parents had already passed away, their siblings were like strangers, and they had no friends. The culture was completely different from what they had been used to, it was all too foreign for them, and assimilating into another unknown was too much for them. When I first heard about things like this, I felt sorry for those missionaries and was glad not to be in their shoes. Until, that is, I realized I was no different from them.

"At least the local people and fellow missionaries here treat me with respect and acknowledge me as a missionary. Surely it's just a matter of attitude. This is my family now; I can laugh with them, cry with them, fight with them, and most of all, love them. To say that I am only here because I don't fit in back in my real home would be a sin. Insofar as God keeps me here, I must embrace it," I thought.

Besides, in Africa I felt useful, knowing I could help people through my ministry, flawed as it, and I, might be. To see newly born-again Christians grow in faith was priceless. In God's eyes, there is absolutely no difference between Korea and Africa. He loves the poor and the rich, the illiterate and literate, the young and old equally. From then on, when people back in Korea praised my work on the mission field, I would accept their encouragement rather than giving the usual polite denial expected by my culture. This was the place I was called to, so here must I stay and work hard until He called me elsewhere. I would be joyful, for in my weakness I was strong.

"Lord, whatever your reasons are, You know I am here for You, to serve You. Please grant me Your power. I am willing to suffer pain and sorrow if it is for You; if this is what you have given me to do, then this is all I want. For Your grace is sufficient for me; through Your grace, You brought this inadequate servant here. I will plant the seeds and may you cause them to grow. Missions is the only thing I can do, Lord, it is the only thing I know. I will do this until You return, my life is worth nothing without You."

12

ME, DEPRESSED?

I am what is called a "people person". Ever since I can remember, I have always liked being surrounded by friends and family. When I was a starving seminary student, my house was always full of other starving seminary students and those times are some of my most enjoyable memories. When I studied in England during the WEC Candidate Orientation Course, my home was once again always bustling with people. It was such a natural part of me, as though God planned it that way as preparation for my life as a missionary.

After years of training my wife and I took our two young daughters and headed to our mission field in Africa. We were pleasantly surprised to find the local people were extremely kind and welcoming. Hosting visitors is a part of everyday life; it is normal to stop by a friend's house and stay for a while, sometimes for a few days. It wasn't necessary to ask ahead of time, which we had to get used to very quickly. As you can imagine, my house was usually alive with young people from the village day in and day out, which created amazing opportunities to share the gospel with them. I was really happy about that. Some of them were very resistant to hearing anything that questioned Islam and never came back. Others, however, responded positively, enabling us to start Bible study groups which eventually grew and formed the Omega Church.

The senior missionaries who had been living there for a long time advised me to be more careful about letting the youth come and go as they liked. What was said did make sense, but I didn't believe it quite applied to me because I was convinced that having the young folks over all the time was the best way for me to share the Word with them.

I liked seeing young people relaxing, reading, playing games and enjoying themselves in my home – in the beginning anyway. But then I felt my attitude begin to change over time, and I found myself growing tired of having them over constantly without any notice or respect for my privacy. I felt suffocated and even resentful of these young people that continuously made my home theirs. I found myself getting annoyed when I walked out of my room and saw them lying around in my living room or chatting in my backyard. What had looked like opportunities for evangelism now seemed like babysitting. I realized a lot of them came hoping to get something from me, whether it was free stationery, food, or anything else they could leave with. I became physically and mentally exhausted. Finally, just hearing the knocking on the door made me stiffen with irritation. "What do they want now? Tell them I'm out," I would say to my wife as she went to the door.

I began to withdraw from everything and felt antisocial. I knew something was wrong with me because this was so unlike me. Was I depressed? I just wanted my space and for no one to bother me. If this morbid aversion I was feeling towards social interaction was really a sign of depression then my ministry was over. That would be it!

I had heard other missionaries speak about similar problems.

The longer they were on the field, the more they longed to be alone. Coming home after a hard day's work and being able to sit in peace and quiet was all they wanted. As soon as it was time for a break, the first thing that came to mind was finding a solitary place to meditate alone and sleep for as long as needed.

Is that what I was feeling? "But I'm not like others, I'm a people person! I'm supposed to like having people around me all the time!" I thought, confused and concerned. In mission work, an essential factor for success lies in building personal relationships. If a missionary can't handle spending time with others, he or she might as well pack up and go home. So I began to think, "All right, if I'm going to be a missionary, I must accept them on all occasions. After all, it's their culture and their lifestyle! To force them to adjust to my style must be wrong. I'm going to have to open my door to them and be happy to see them anytime. That's why God sent me here. As a matter of fact, I should go visit them before they even come to me! I am done with you, depression! Get away from me!"

I patted my tired face and went outside to look at the beautiful night sky. Millions of twinkling stars speckled the sky and reminded me of the way the eyes of the people here sparkle with innocence and genuine joy. "Lord, may I watch over them as these stars are watching over me now. Forgive me for the way I have been. Surely my depression has left me now. God, I was foolish and it will never happen to me again as long as I am here," I prayed silently as I looked up at the glistening moon.

"Mr. Yoo, look how many stars are up there," I heard a voice say. I saw that three local youths had joined me and were now happily smiling at the sky.

Apparently stargazing in peace was not an option. I instantly felt my jaw clench and my neck tighten. I managed a smile, or what looked more like an awkward lip curl displaying my upper teeth before I slipped back into my house.

"Yup, still depressed," I muttered.

PART II

HOPE AND DISAPPOINTMENT

13

MY ONESIMUS IN PRISON

Prison outreach was one of my ministries. There were two prisons so I was extremely busy on Sunday visiting both of them in the same afternoon. I was working with another local pastor from a nearby church who had gotten permission from the government for us to preach to these prisoners. Their reasoning was that they believed the prisoners could be changed if they adopted a new religion that promoted good works and peace. This was an incredible opportunity for us as we were able to minister to many prisoners. Actually, quite a number of them accepted Jesus and became completely transformed. One good example is Kalifa, who is now a great pastor in one of our local churches.

It seemed as though the prisoners were more open to the gospel than other people. If not eager to hear the sermon, they at least were anxious to get out of their cells for a moment even if it meant listening to a Christian pastor. There was no chapel so we used a small classroom in the prison that could only fit fifty people. The prisoners would hurry to take a seat otherwise they were not let in. I knew that not all of them were really interested in what I had to say but I was grateful that I had them all in the room so they could have the opportunity to hear the Word and sing praise songs that might linger in their minds.

A young man named Ansu used to interpret my sermons in one

of the local languages. I was still learning the different dialects and could understand pretty well but couldn't quite speak fluently, so I was more comfortable with someone translating for me. Fortunately, Ansu was fluent in English and in quite a few other languages so this was tremendously helpful for me. There were also prisoners who were natives of neighboring countries who had been caught trafficking drugs locally. Ansu was even able to communicate with them. He was also very open about being a Christian and would confidently declare his faith in front of his fellow inmates. Ansu was a gifted man.

He was released from prison earlier than his original sentence because of good behavior. The prison officers stated that he had been a good role model to other prisoners and were reassured by his dedication to Sunday service. They believed him to be sincere in his transformation and wished him luck in his new beginning. Ansu came to my house as soon as he was discharged from prison. I welcomed him warmly and arranged for him to stay with one of the youth center staff members. He had helped me so much in prison, I was excited to see what he would do now that he was out. He regularly attended Sunday services and Bible study. No one doubted his faith.

One day, the worker he was staying with told me that things were being stolen from him. He was convinced that Ansu was the thief but I scolded him for being so quick to accuse Ansu just because he was an ex-convict. Soon enough, Ansu was caught red-handed and I was stunned. He had been stealing small household goods and selling them. This made no sense because they were of hardly any value. I didn't understand why Ansu had done this. I had been so sure he was a changed man after getting out of prison. Before I could even get an explanation from him, he disappeared. I felt numb more than anything; I had gone through this before and decided that I needed to just let him go.

Prison ministry became very difficult after that. I no longer had Ansu by my side and desperately needed someone to translate my sermons into the different dialects. I found people to replace him but no one could do it as well as Ansu did. On some occasions, the interpreter would intentionally change my sermons, using Mohammed's name instead of Jesus. At other times the interpreter would simply refuse to translate what I was saying, for example when I taught about Jesus being equal to God. I tried to work with quite a few translators but went though the same problems with them all. Consequently, my messages grew longer and longer and started to get lost in incorrect translations. Weeks, months went by, and I could never feel at ease as I preached because I was worried about the accuracy of the translations, especially when I taught on sensitive issues that depended on absolute clarity.

One Sunday afternoon, I was having a particularly difficult time with the translator because he continued to distort what I was saying. Suddenly, one of the prisoners stood up and marched to the interpreter. "If you're going to translate for him then, for crying out loud, do it right!" he said angrily and pushed the other inmate aside. Surprised, I took a closer look at this disheveled fellow who was now standing by me but wouldn't make eye contact. His hair was tangled and his dirty beard was hiding his haggard face. It was Ansu! I couldn't believe how much his appearance had changed and couldn't find the words to say. I quietly continued my sermon and he proceeded to translate with the same ease and confidence as he used to. I immediately felt a burden being lifted off of my shoulders and couldn't help but smile throughout the rest of my message.

Neither of us said a word after service. We didn't have to; it was as though we already knew what the other was thinking. He stood there silently staring at his feet as I packed up my things. His expression was filled with shame and remorse; this was a broken man standing before me silently seeking comfort from his only outside connection to God. I never asked him how he ended up back in jail. I found out later that he had actually been back in jail for a couple months before he could muster up the courage to come to service. When he finally did come, the first few times he had sat at the back, hidden by the other inmates.

I felt incredibly happy as I drove home that day. It wasn't because I didn't have to worry about my sermons anymore. I reflected back on the first time Ansu ever gave his testimony in prison, "I was lost when I was free and have found life locked up in prison. I have met my Lord Jesus Christ and I am truly blessed."

"Yes, Ansu, you met your Savior in prison and now you can work for Him in prison. From now on, we will work together once again for the good news of Christ. You are my partner in prison!" I spoke out aloud as if Ansu could hear me back in the prison.

Now that I had Ansu back, I felt all the confidence that had drained out of me seep back in. I had him by my side and I felt strong. I would speak and Ansu would relay the message with enthusiasm and passion. Sometimes his words were more powerful than mine and fueled the atmosphere of worship with great energy.

My heart went out to Ansu as I thought of his life. He had had a difficult past and couldn't manage to stay out of jail. I could easily understand how the hardships of his outside world had only made it easier for him to fail and eventually pushed him back behind prison walls. "If many prisoners' lives are changed when they hear the gospel through you, then it is worthwhile, Ansu," I thought. As much as I benefited from his being in prison, of course, I can't say that God put Ansu in prison for my sake. But one thing I know for certain is that everything works out for the good of those who love Him. Ansu had become my co-worker in prison preaching the gospel. He was my Onesimus.

14

BLIND PARTNERS IN ACTION

One day a young man from the T— tribe arrived at my church. His given name was Saki Tourang, but he had changed his name to Steven after becoming a Christian. It was rare to win a soul for Christ, so I was very pleased to see him in our house church. Frankly speaking, I couldn't bring myself to ask him how he had become a Christian because if he told me that he had attended another house church, I would appear to be stealing a sheep from someone else. It was better not to know.

Steven regularly attended the church services and participated well in praying with us. One day he asked me to write a verification of his attendance. Steven diligently came to church so there was no reason not to give him what he asked for, but he offered no explanation about why he wanted it. After he obtained the attendance record, he only occasionally returned to the services.

But no secrets exist in Africa. I soon found out his story. One day he had been walking along the beach and had met a good-hearted European couple. After talking with them, he proclaimed that he would believe in Jesus even though he was from a Muslim background. The European couple was so excited. After their return to their country, they continued their contact with him in writing, and providing money towards any need that he shared.

Steven showed great skill in touching the hearts and interest of this couple and, later, their extended church family. Some of his correspondence let their church know that he had lost his job because he was now a Christian. He also shared that he was ostracized by his family and had to beg door to door to make a living. The church members in Europe raised funds for the persecuted young Steven, and even sent a representative to Africa to see what else they could do to provide aid for the long run rather than just meeting Steven's present financial need. The representative took stock of the situation and suggested that Steven purchase an orchard. The church monies were used to acquire land, fence a garden, and purchase some nursery trees.

During the following year the European church regularly sent him financial support. Steven continued to touch their hearts with his letters and reports of progress including photos of the growing orchard. The trouble with his correspondence, though, was that none of the information was true. He was only twenty-five years old, but smart enough to cheat these good-hearted church members. He had not lost his job, because, for a fact, he had never been employed. He was not ostracized by his family. He did not continue with the orchard but sent pictures of another orchard to show trees growing.

These church members were sacrificing financially to give from their hard-earned money while Steven used all of their money for his own pleasure. If they had only asked a missionary on the field for some advice, they would not have wasted God's money for so many years. Wanting to help, but spiritually blind, they committed a folly without even recognizing it. God must have looked down and thought, "What foolish people!"

One day I heard that another couple from the European church had come to visit Steven. This couple was also taken in by his lies and took photos to show back home. It was deplorable that they didn't try to meet local church members, come to my church where Steven said he attended, or try to learn more about his faith, friends, and fellowship. Whatever reasons they may have had, they didn't ask to meet anyone else before they departed.

Steven's lie did not last forever. A big argument occurred among his accomplices and a friend revealed his lie. But it was too late for the European church. The offerings raised with tears by the church had already been used by this young man.

Probably there are many other blind supporters out there who send money to other Stevens without using God's servants in the field to make sure the money is being well invested. The blindness of this kind-hearted church began when it so lightly believed that a local native, met briefly on vacation, would convert and grow without any real evidence of long-term commitments and connection to a local church. On several visits to Africa, the supporters were so pleased with their personal arm of fellowship connecting with Steven that they never shared fellowship with the local church that was supposedly helping him grow. This blindness led them to invest for years in a single person, without any networking with others supposedly playing a role in his life also.

Count how many believers in Christ missionaries have won so far. In Africa, the numbers have been few in areas that have resisted penetration by the gospel. Count those faithful missionaries who burned with youthful passion for these people despite the hot sun, who loved them, shared the gospel with them whenever there was an opportunity, prayed for patients, dressed their wounds, and so on. If it were possible to win souls by simply talking with a stranger on the beach, then the missionaries would have many more churches to show for their efforts on these difficult mission fields. Some may think my words sound bitter and critical, but as a servant on the mission field, I want to speak candidly to this difficult situation

I was sick of the endless efforts in this spiritually dark land where no strategy seemed to work. There is a hidden spiritual power behind those pure and simple eyes that keeps these nationals resistant. I found it difficult to relate to the European church which felt conversion was so easy. Are there really chosen people here? Or are they all like Steven? I felt guilty for being a missionary who harbored thoughts like that.

Once again I renewed my mind in prayer and embraced the souls lost in the darkness with new hope. The way will open; I strongly began to believe God's Word again. Stubborn hearts will be broken and the door for the gospel will be opened wide. " 'Not by might nor by power, but by my Spirit', says the LORD Almighty." *(Zechariah 4)*. "Lift up your heads, O you gates ... that the King of glory may come in." *(Psalm24)*. Jesus, the King of glory! There is no one to shut the doors. O Lord, open the doors! Please open the doors for your servant who feels discouraged.

15

CULTURE VERSUS BIBLE

This country does not allow foreigners to reside here as missionaries so one can only obtain a long-term visa under the premise of business or social welfare projects. So, we began a vocational training program for young women, teaching them how to type. It started off as a small-scale typing class with only ten typewriters, classes in the morning and evening. Twenty young ladies enrolled and the classes went very well. Though we didn't pressure them to become Christians, some of them chose to attend Sunday worship which was wonderful.

My wife and I got to know two teenage girls pretty well. Patim and Musi had been close friends since childhood. They begged me to put them in the same class which I did. They regularly attended Sunday services for over a year and even volunteered to help out during Sunday School. They both were a great joy to me and I cared for them like my own. I truly believed they had accepted Jesus as their Savior so I decided to go forward with their baptism.

But not too long after their baptism preparations started, I discovered that Musi had gotten pregnant even though she was only seventeen years old. This is actually quite common here but seeing that she was a member of my church, I could not ignore it. Musi tried to hide it from us knowing what we would say, but

Patim had already told me. There was no choice for me but to remove her name from the baptism ceremony list. After that, she stopped coming to church and typing school all together.

A few months later, I was told that Musi gave birth to a daughter. I was torn as to what to do. I wanted to visit her to see how she was doing yet, as a pastor of her church, I did not want it to seem that I was condoning what she had done. After all, I was tremendously disappointed and, truthfully, I wanted her to know that. I never went to visit Musi; I was told later that she was very angry because although both she and Patim had done wrong, only she had suffered the consequences of their behavior. I confronted Patim who was just weeks away from being baptized but Patim adamantly denied everything and said she didn't know why Musi wanted to bring her down like this.

I decided to move on with everything, and Patim completed her baptism course. She publicly confessed her faith and was baptized during a lovely ceremony. I was so excited and shared her story with my prayer partners back at home. What a challenge this young girl had overcome! She was raised a Muslim and now had become baptized as a daughter of Christ. She was also now old enough to be a great bridal candidate for the young men at church. It was always so hard to find good, Christian wives for the fellows as not too many young ladies were able to come to church. Patim talked excitedly about someday being the one and only wife of a nice Christian young man. I always wanted to bring together new Christian couples and help them grow as a family who could then set an example for others around them. I was very pleased with the way things were going although Musi always stayed in the back of my mind. Before long, the time for our furlough came and we left for a year. Wishing them all the best until I would return, I left, excited to see how things would have changed when I came back.

On our return after the year of furlough, I was surprised to find that Patim no longer came to church. Of course, Musi was not there either but I had not expected to see her. I thought maybe Patim wasn't satisfied with the local pastor who had taken over my ministry while I was gone. I asked around about Patim's whereabouts and found out her new address. When my wife and I got to her house, she was bathing a little baby only a few months old. We hadn't heard anything about her getting married so we figured it must be her nephew. While we were all catching up, however, the baby started crying, upon which Patim began to breastfeed him. Stunned, I asked, "Whose baby is this?" She just smiled and kept looking at her son in silence.

Patim had become the *fourth wife* of a man during our furlough. It turns out that she had actually gotten pregnant right before we left the country. This husband of hers, however, had moved to Europe and was living with a white woman he had met there.

"Whatever happened to all that talk about wanting to marry a nice Christian young man and being his only wife? Did you not say yourself that you would never be a second or third wife? But then you got pregnant and became the fourth wife of some man who didn't even care enough to stay here with you and your child?" I asked exasperated.

I felt cold sweat drip down my back as I stood up. I was so greatly disappointed that I felt as though all my strength had left me. What did I do wrong as a pastor that this was happening to me? I knew this was a normal aspect of their culture but I had thought maybe I could make a difference with Patim. How foolish I felt as I thought about how pleased I had been thinking up all these dreams for Patim, not knowing she already had that man's baby in her womb.

Patim didn't say anything but just sat there. My wife looked at the baby in silence and quietly stood up with no expression. Patim's eyes seemed to say that she knew how we felt and that she was sorry. She didn't move as we walked out. Though no words were spoken, we knew we wouldn't see her again for a long time.

A little over a year later, as I walked down the street, I ran into a lady who looked to be in her middle age. She was carrying an infant on her back with a little boy clinging to her finger. She spoke to me like she recognized me so I took a closer look. It was Patim! She looked so much older than she really was. Anyone would agree that she easily looked as though she was in her late thirties, even though she was barely into her twenties. Glancing at the baby girl on her back, I asked, "Did her father come back from Europe?"

She told me that he was still in Europe and had never come back. She never heard from him but it was all right, she said, because she had completely forgotten about him now. I didn't want to ask her who the father of this baby was. It was better that I didn't know, I thought. We stood there for a moment in an awkward silence but I knew I couldn't let her just walk away. I smiled as I gently patted the squirmy little boy's head. This was just part of their culture, this was normal so I simple had to accept it. Why had I been so harsh with my judgments? This was all they knew. Patim and Musi weren't the only ones who were in these situations; it was simply a natural part of the lives of many young girls here. I took Patim's hands in mine and asked her if she was willing to give the life of faith another shot. All of a sudden, her face stiffened and her expression grew stern. She could have easily said "yes" like most of them do when I ask them to stick to their faith, but she stood there with her lips sealed together.

I couldn't blame her. How could she act otherwise? The last time she had been rejected and forced to live a difficult, lonely life, the only thing I had done was criticize her and show her I was disappointed in her. I had judged her by my own standards and my strict cultural perspective, rather than trying to understand her and her environment like Jesus would have done. He would have understood that indeed she had made a mistake. She had had her youth taken from her and her future ruined, yet no one cared because this happened all the time. At that moment, I realized that she must have been deeply hurt when the very people who taught her forgiveness and love walked away from her that day.

As I dragged my feet home, I wondered why I hadn't been more understanding. As difficult as it would have been, why hadn't I opened my arms to her and her little baby from the beginning? I didn't know if I'd ever completely understand the people here and their culture. On the one hand, I wanted so much for the people of my church to pursue a life of righteousness, following the way of the Bible. On the other hand, I felt as though I had lost two precious souls, Patim and Musi, all because of my criticism and arrogant view of their culture.

So many times mission work feels like a mangled knot I have no idea how to untangle.

16

WHATEVER HAPPENED TO MY COMPASSION?

The first language I learned upon arrival to the field was the main tribal language. However, after our first furlough my family was assigned to do ministry with another tribe, so we had to learn their language as well. We decided to move to a small village far away in the countryside in hopes that we would learn the language more quickly as no one spoke English there.

Lam and Jean were still in school so we had to leave them with another family who agreed to take care of them until our language study was over. Taking only our youngest who was still just a toddler, we left our sobbing daughters and promised them we would be back to see them soon. Our new home was truly in the middle of the country where most of the residents had no electricity or running water. At night, the sound of the wild animals was so loud that sometimes it seemed like they were walking around in our house. I'll always remember how the hyenas would shriek and howl as they fought over a dead animal. "Wow, we're really living in Africa," my wife would say.

In the other room, Yevon was sleeping away, completely unaware of what was going on outside. As we expected, she adapted easily and went about as if she was born in the village. She played happily with the local children, rolling about freely in the dirt (and sometimes eating it). She blended in quite nicely with her surroundings – literally.

Yevon got along really well with all the villagers but she was particularly fond of Sofia, a lady who lived alone next door to us in the same compound. I was told that her husband lived in another country and I never asked any questions about it. Sofia loved Yevon and went everywhere with Yevon tied around her back. Because of her good relationship with Yevon, my wife and I got to know her very well and treated her like family. Sofia was an amazing cook and often brought us food she had made. We often walked to the local market together to get ingredients for dinner and she would cook for us when we got home. Then we would huddle around a large bowl full of steaming rice and sauce, eating with our hands and talking together.

I often saw unfamiliar men in the compound who had come to visit Sofia. They would walk into her home and come out some time later. Culturally, it is very common and acceptable to walk into a friend's bedroom to chat and visit with them so I thought nothing of it. One day, my language tutor mentioned that he had something to tell me. He said that he was concerned about Yevon spending so much time with Sofia. "Why? Sofia's a lovely young lady!" I said. "Sofia's a prostitute," he said quickly. I was shocked. Then it all made sense why all those men were coming in and out of her house all the time. I couldn't believe that I hadn't put that all together earlier but I was more shocked by the fact that there was a prostitute in such a remote village.

I hate to say it, but everything changed after that and I couldn't look at her the same way anymore. It wasn't that she was a prostitute that bothered me – or maybe it was, I don't know. All I knew was that suddenly, I felt very uncomfortable around Sofia and couldn't act normal around her. Thoughts began rushing through my mind as I remembered reading a report about AIDS having increased dramatically in Africa killing millions. "What if Sofia has AIDS? Is Yevon safe around a prostitute?" I wondered as I paced around my room.

We didn't share meals with Sofia anymore. Yevon didn't understand what was going on and often cried, asking why we couldn't eat with Sofia. Sofia didn't understand what was happening either. She thought that maybe we stopped eating with her because we didn't like her cooking anymore. She began to spend a longer time in the kitchen, pouring her heart and soul into cooking a better meal. She continued to bring over food and ask for Yevon only to hear a polite excuse from us. We couldn't find the right words to confront her, making the situation more and more awkward. The more we withdrew, the harder she tried.

Reluctantly, I told the landlord about her being a prostitute. I was not comfortable knowing that prostitution was going on in the next house I said. And what about my daughter? I didn't want her to be exposed to such things I continued. If she didn't leave, then I would move my family I told him. "Why of course! We cannot have that kind of depravity here!" the landlord huffed angrily as he marched towards Sofia's home. This was how the conversation between a heartless coward and his landlord ended.

That night, Sofia packed her belongings. Yevon whined and kept pleading for me to let her go see Sofia. "Well, we should let Yevon see her one last time," I said to my wife and so we went to Sofia's to say good-bye. When I saw the sadness etched on Sofia's face, feelings of guilt, pity, and hopelessness overwhelmed me. What had I done? I lowered my head as I could not look at her in the eyes. With a burning conscience I thought, "How could I, a servant of my Lord who was a loving friend to those labeled unlovable and unforgivable, do this to Sofia? And I'm supposed to be a missionary? This was the best I could do for her? And because of what, because I thought she *might* have AIDS? So what if she did?" I cannot quite put to words the tremendous regret and shame that clenched my heart that night as I watched Sofia smooth Yevon's hair, loving tears filling her eyes as she walked away.

I saw Sofia some months later in the marketplace. She was so thin and looked as though she had aged twenty years. I had heard that she was sick but no one knew from what. I didn't know what to say to her. As I walked home that afternoon, I wondered what Jesus would say to me if he were here. The tears started to flow as I heard Him say, "I have sent you here to comfort the poor and the sick. I have sent you here to love them and save the lost but instead, look how you pushed this woman away. I lived among lepers and washed feet, but what about you? You let your ignorant fear get the better of you and sent her away without even sharing the gospel with her – you sent her away from Me." I felt broken and deeply ashamed by my own behavior; till this day, I am not sure if I have ever forgiven myself for that.

Some time later, I was told that Sofia suffered from her illness for a long time before she died. No one knows what exactly she died from.

17

DO YOU HEAR MY CRYING?

A young man named Arum was a regular member of our church. Amiable and very intelligent, he learned the Word easily and developed a solid understanding of the gospel. After he was baptized, he wanted to make sure his younger sister, Fati, was saved and brought her to church one morning. Fati had just finished secondary school and was still in her mid teens. She was an exceptionally pretty girl who turned many heads wherever she went. Despite the continuous attention she received for her looks, she was unusually humble and had a kind, gentle heart. All the church members adored her and spoke very highly of her. She attended service with her brother every Sunday and became a committed member of the church. She had completed her baptism classes and continued to grow in her faith.

Just as her brother Arum had been castigated by his family, it was now Fati's turn, except it was worse this time. Once a Muslim woman confesses her faith in Christ, she must be prepared for severe persecution and even death. Her parents were not yet aware of her conversion because they lived in a rural village far away. Her grandfather and her uncle, on the other hand, were furious and kept a close watch over her. Determined to keep coming to church, Fati managed to come up with excuses that allowed her to leave her house.

I enrolled her as a typing student in the center so she could give her relatives a valid reason for coming to the center. This started out well and she was able to come to church anytime on the pretext of the typing class. She diligently continued to attend services, Bible study, and even became a devoted Sunday School teacher. But of course there are no secrets here. We could not keep her attendance hidden because of the many "watchdog" neighbors who kept an eye on her at the request of her relatives. Eventually, news of her new faith reached her parents in her hometown.

Fati came to us one day and told me her parents had called her home immediately. When she saw the concern on my face, she smiled and assured us that everything would be all right and that she would be back after a few days. Weeks and months went by and Fati didn't return. I knew something was wrong so I sent her brother to their hometown to find out what was going on. Days later, Arum came back with bags under his eyes and a grim look on his face.

He sat down and began to recount everything that had happened. His parents had let Fati live in the city after graduating from secondary school so she could pursue further studies. When they found out she spent all her time in a Christian church instead, they were incensed that she could dishonor them that way. She had lost her soul to this "Christian nonsense" and had brought great shame to the family. Before she could make her family look any worse, they decided to sell her to one of her father's friends, well into his sixties, as a third wife. Now, she was forbidden to leave her hometown. As a matter of fact, she might as well have been caged in her new home. I felt rage well up within me at the thought of young, innocent, kind Fati forced to live under the control of a man old enough to be her grandfather. How could her parents do this? I shouldn't have sent her home. I paced around the living room, jaw clenched with bitterness, as Arum sat hunched over in his chair, silently staring at the floor.

What kind of dark, ugly power does this religion have that it possesses a father to sell his own daughter into such a dreadful life? And what would happen when her old husband passed away? She would be a young widow, left out like yesterday's paper. News would spread that she had been sold as a third wife because she had betrayed her family's religion, so who would want to marry her? I felt as though my stomach was caving in as I thought about how brightly Fati would smile as she talked about marrying one Christian man and taking care of her family. Now the worst had happened to her and that dream of hers was heartlessly snatched away.

I felt as though it was my fault. If I had helped her become even stronger in her faith, could she have gotten out of this circumstance? Though I prayed for her, would the situation get any easier for her? Fati, if you can hear me, hold on to your strength, Fati. Pray to the Lord for courage. A door will open for you, have faith! Do you remember how joyfully you answered my questions during baptism classes? Those answers were your confession of faith. They will save your life.

All of us cried out to God, but Fati never came back. Years later, Arum brought us news about his sister. She had run away under the cover of night with a young man in her village who had promised to take her away from her misery and give her a better life. They fled to a neighboring country and were supposedly now living there together. That was all Arum knew.

Fati, if you can hear me, I'm just glad you're still alive. You must remember the gospel seed that was planted in your heart. No matter where you are and what you're doing, don't forget the wonderful truth that you are His beloved daughter. Though your parents abandoned you, your Father in heaven will never leave you. He is still waiting for you with open arms. You must never let go of this truth. I am still praying for you. I don't know, Fati, if you think it was a blessing that you came to know us and meet Jesus, or a curse. For us, knowing you was an incredible blessing.

18

CURSED WITH POVERTY

My wife and I got to know a young man named Banding well during our ministry. We first met him when he was a young boy, right out of primary school. Since then, he had been a frequent visitor at our home and a regular member of our church. Sensitive and introverted, he had a meek spirit that made me feel especially protective of him. As a young boy, he was terrified of his family's acrimonious opposition to his attending church. Even though his peers at church went on to become baptized, he hesitated because he was too frightened to tell his family.

Years went by and Banding grew up to be a tall, handsome young man. Perhaps the years matured him; he finally came to me asking to be baptized and I was ecstatic. This was his first step of courage as a Christian man and I couldn't wait to see what God would make of him.

Soon after his baptism, Banding got a job which kept him working on Sundays. It was difficult to accept because I knew this would take a toll on his growing faith. Even so, I couldn't stop him because finding alternative employment would be incredibly difficult and I knew his family desperately needed him to work. When he did get days off, he would always come to service which I was grateful for. I didn't want him to fall away from the Lord.

He started to bring a girl named Silvi with him whenever he

could come to church. Silvi had never been to church or even known what church was. She came from an extremely poor family and, to make the story short, she and Banding fell in love. He had supported her during her last year of secondary school and had recently proposed to her. Both families were very pleased and they were set to get married once Banding became a bit more financially stable.

Every year as soon as the Muslim fast is over there is a huge festival. This is one of the greatest events of the entire year. The local people scrounge up any money they have (or borrow some) to buy the best clothes, artificial hair, accessories, and the finest of foods that they will only get to enjoy this one time. Of course, young people especially look forward to this festival because they get to dress up, go to big feasts and meet new people.

Silvi pulled out all the money she had saved throughout the year and bought herself a new dress and the most popular accessory among young people here, non-prescription eyeglasses. With her fashionable frames on, she went to a party at her friend's house.

At the party, Silvi met a young man named Antom. He was tall, sophisticated, and looked rich. He even had a car. Of course, he had borrowed the car from his manager at the nice tourist hotel where he worked as a bell boy. Silvi and Antom hit it off and ended up spending the entire time at the party with each other. He later offered to drive her home, and she happily agreed. When they pulled up to Silvi's home in a fancy car, her parents seemed very interested in Antom. Obviously, to them, this was a great opportunity for their daughter and they immediately offered to give her to him as a wife.

Antom was already married so Silvi would have to be his second wife. Her parents didn't mind, as long as she could be taken care of by this man with a nice car and a job working for white people. Even though she was already engaged, Silvi didn't seem against the idea either. Sure enough, as is always the case, news about a man in a fancy car who brought Silvi home quickly reached Banding who rushed over to her house to see what the commotion was all about. He convinced Silvi that Antom could never love her as much as he did, no matter how much money he had. She agreed and told him that she would stay with him. Banding decided they needed to get married right away and went to talk to her parents about it.

Back when Banding had bought them a bottle of the finest oil and paid for their daughter's tuition with his paychecks, Silvi's parents had treated him like a son-in-law. After meeting Antom, however, they changed their minds and decided that Banding was no longer the right man for Silvi to marry. Banding was simply too poor, they said. Sadly enough, even though she had promised to stay with Banding, Silvi began to change her mind as well. Rides in Antom's borrowed car increased while time with Banding became more and more sparse.

Banding's desperate efforts to win Silvi back were futile as her parents wanted nothing more to do with him and always sent Silvi on errands with Antom. Heartbroken, Banding grew bitter and deeply resentful of Silvi, her parents, and his own poverty. He stopped eating and sleeping, completely withdrawing from everyone.

He came to see me one day, his eyes bloodshot and face swollen. Something wasn't right. He didn't say anything but he looked ill. I encouraged him to stop thinking about Silvi. With time, he would forget about her and meet another lovely young lady, I assured him. Our annual Easter camp was coming up, where he could get his mind off her. I suggested he take time off from work to come, relax, and have meaningful fellowship with other young people his age. I asked my assistant, Ali, to take special care of Banding and make sure to help him take his mind off his troubles.

The camp seemed to do nothing for Banding. He would just stay in bed, isolated and miserable. No matter how hard anyone tried, he refused to participate in anything and wanted to go home.

I wanted to spend more time with him but I was incredibly busy during and after camp so I didn't get to check up on how he was doing. On my way to a conference, Ali told me that Banding had been taken to the hospital because he was having trouble breathing. "That poor boy is lovesick," I thought and sent Ali to the hospital on my behalf to encourage Banding. Meetings, seminars, moving, and other matters kept me preoccupied so I planned on going to visit Banding after he got discharged from the hospital. In the meantime, I was worried about him so I asked Sambo, a worker I knew at the hospital, to keep me updated on Banding's progress.

Late one Sunday night after a meeting, I visited Silvi's home because I knew she was the only one that could make him feel better. Without making any small talk, I sat her down and got right to the point. "Are you going marry a man or money? Think carefully," I asked her. She told me that yes, she may have gotten carried away for a moment but she really did love Banding but couldn't say anything because of her parents. Determined to make things right for Banding, I went to talk to Silvi's parents. I encouraged (begged is probably the more appropriate verb here) them to rethink their decision to give Silvi to Antom. "He knew she was engaged and still pursued her. That doesn't sound like an honorable man to me. Listen, he's already married. Are you going to just let him swoop in here with his manager's car and take your precious daughter as a second wife? What if he finds another lady down the road? What'll become of Silvi then? You know Banding is a good man. He gave up so much for your daughter because he loves her. He may be poor now but he's hardworking and trustworthy. You know he'll always take care of your daughter. If money's the only issue here, I'll help him in any way I can." They looked at me inquisitively for a while and spoke to each other quietly. After what seemed like hours, they said that they also wanted Silvi to be happy and decided against giving her to Antom as long as she wanted to be with Banding. Everyone seemed happy with their decision. I was excited to tell my wife and, of course, Banding!

Before I could even tell Banding, I received news from Sambo that Banding was in a critical condition so my wife and I rushed to the hospital to see him early the next morning. To our despair, we were too late. Without ever hearing the good news, he had passed away in the middle of the night. The nurse told us he had had a seizure, spitting out blood before he died in pain. I was stunned and horrified that he had died so tragically and without anyone by his side, especially the one he wanted to be there the most. Unable to handle my sorrow and guilt, I couldn't stay there any longer.

What would I say to him when I saw him in heaven? How would I look him in the eye after not even visiting him in the hospital and nurturing him back to health? I had been too busy to even realize he was dying alone. Would he ever forgive this foolish pastor? My youngest daughter Yevon sobbed on the ground when we told her that Banding was no longer with us. He had always doted on little Yevon and she adored him. It was the first time we had lost someone so close to us on the field and the thought of Banding still brings tears to my eyes.

As was his wish, Banding's body was taken back to his hometown in the countryside to be buried. I sat in his small room for a long time in silence, wishing that I could turn back time. On my way out, I ran into Silvi who looked as if she had been crying for hours. She collapsed into my arms and wept uncontrollably as if she blamed herself for Banding's death. Poverty was her curse. Poverty was Banding's curse.

"This must be really hard for you. Banding has left us now, and I hope you'll be able to move on and search for a new life without him. Don't let yourself be consumed by his death or you'll never be free from it." As I encouraged her, I knew in the back of my mind the way things would unfold now that Banding was gone.

"This is Allah's will, Mr. Yoo. Don't you see? Allah never wanted me to be with Banding. That is why he gave me Antom, and Banding has gone. I can only follow Allah's will and marry Antom, even if I have to be his second wife. I know there will be other wives but what can I do? That is my fate destined by Allah. I am just a human and cannot change that."

As she spoke, I felt a part of my heart turn cold with resentment. I couldn't believe those words were coming out of her mouth the day Banding was buried, and in his own home. Blinded by her faith in her god, it was as though she had buried her love for Banding with him – almost like his death was now meaningless because it was simply the will of Allah. I was once again reminded of the darkness that has taken hold of the people here. I feel so small, Lord, help me.

19

TEENAGE STEP-MOM

The intricate customs and traditional processes behind marriage in Africa are relatively difficult to keep track of. Each tribe seems to do things differently with its own set of requirements and procedures that each member must absolutely follow. For example, my next door neighbor Karam had yet to be married even though he had been engaged for ten years. His poor bride-to-be was still waiting for him to be able to afford the dowry for his bride. He asked me to loan him money which I simply didn't have. Marriage customs here are complicated and binding. Though I lived there for many years, I never understood most of them.

Ndong and his brother, Jakar, were two young fellows that attended my church. They lived with their large family which included their uncle, Aziz (their father's younger brother), who happened to be the same age as Ndong. Their family is from a tribe that usually encourages a man to have many wives, but Ndong and Jakar's father had only one wife for a very long time. He was from a village in the countryside and often went back to visit.

One day, the father came back excited about a gift he had brought from home: his sixteen-year-old niece. He showed her off happily to the family like he had bought a nice calf from the market place. There, it is common to treat girls like possessions that you can gift back and forth. Marriages within the extended family are relatively common and, apparently, Ndong's father's cousin decided to give his daughter who was "now the marrying age" as a gift to Ndong's family.

Turning away a gift from a family member was unacceptable, so Ndong's father willingly received his cousin's gift. The girl was homely and illiterate but he was quite pleased nonetheless because he believed that this new addition to the family would take the load off his wife, who had to take care of him, his brother Aziz, and his five sons. He thought he could give the girl to twenty-two-year-old Aziz to have as his wife but he would have to consult the whole family first. The family gathered for a meeting to decide which person would benefit the most from having the girl as his new wife. First priority went to Aziz.

This would be a good opportunity for Aziz to get a wife without having to pay a dowry but Aziz refused. He didn't like the girl because he thought she wasn't pretty and was uneducated. He remarked that he still felt too young and was definitely not ready to marry. A little thrown off his original plan, the father went to his eldest son, Ndong, and asked him to marry her instead. Ndong refused as well. He had graduated from high school, gained a lot of experience in the working world, and was unwilling to marry an illiterate girl who hadn't even gone to elementary school. As much as he didn't want to dishonor his father by disobeying him, he simply would not marry her.

Ndong's father had to do something. He was the head of the household so he was going to make the decision alone from here on, he said. The young bride was given to Ndong's younger brother, Jakar. Jakar was stunned but was too frightened to refuse his father's wishes. He was only seventeen and still in ninth grade. He reluctantly agreed as he really had no choice. The notion of marriage had never yet crossed his mind and now it was decided that he would marry this distant relative he had never met before. He was sad and scared about his future. Jakar came to me one evening, with tears of anguish in his eyes, and told me the story about what had happened. I knew I had to do something.

I went to see Ndong and Jakar's father first thing the next morning and sat down to seriously discuss his son's upcoming marriage. I pleaded with him and convinced him not to dampen his young son's future by making him marry. Jakar still had to finish high school and had so much potential. If he had a wife and possibly children to worry about, this young boy would have to give up everything and start working so he could support his family. Jakar's father didn't put up a fight and agreed with me. He already knew everything I was telling him. He knew it would be a big mistake to give a wife to a young boy who hadn't the slightest clue about marriage or raising a family. He finally decided to call off the whole thing.

But now he was in trouble. His sons wouldn't take the girl and it would damage his relationship with his relatives if he returned the girl to her home. According to custom, when you are given a relative as a gift and you reject that gift, it means you are breaking your relationship with that family. Well, the girl wasn't going to be his sister-in-law, first daughter-in-law, or second daughter-in-law, so she was going to have to be his second wife! Imagine the whole picture: a man in his fifties takes a sixteen-year-old girl as his second wife. As bizarre as it sounds, it really wasn't an unusual scenario. The most interesting part of this situation was that Ndong and Jakar now had to call their sixteen-year-old cousin, "Mother".

20

AREN'T YOU SUPPOSED TO LOVE US?

If you were to sit a dozen local young men down and ask them what their biggest dream was, almost all of them would say, "To go overseas and make a lot of money!" And then they would smile and continue, "And to marry a white woman, get citizenship in her country, and then move back here!" The economic structure (or lack thereof) has created a chasm in the employment world and made it incredibly difficult for even the educated to find solid jobs here. Thus, marrying a white woman has become the most desirable solution to getting ahead in life.

It works out quite well for these desperate fellows that a lot of older, single ladies come here on vacation. As a result, large crowds of young men in their barely-there swim-trunks loiter around the beaches by hotels, especially during the tourist season. Finding that white woman is their main goal. They could wait for days, even for months, if it means finding that woman who will be the one to turn their lives around.

There were four boys in the Chuki family: Lang, Shul, Sere and Kaw. One hot afternoon, Lang ran into an older Norwegian lady walking along the shore. They met and she later paid for a house to be built for his family. You don't get much luckier than that. His brother, Sere, also spent his days on the beach and found himself a German lady who later bought a nice car for him that he used for work as a taxi driver. The youngest, Kaw, befriended an older British lady who paid his way through secondary school. Shul was the only one in his family who hadn't found a walking money bag in the form of a white woman. Needless to say, he spent every waking moment at the beach.

This scenario is rather common and often enough you see such couples, a young local fellow and his older white girlfriend or wife. There is a small coastal village a couple of hours away from our home. Twenty-two young men from this one village have managed to find European wives and moved to Europe with them. This village is a single example; imagine how many more men from here are now living in Europe. Free homes, free cars, easy money, and you even get to live where the white folks live! What a dream; such a simple solution! So how can anyone blame these boys for seeing white women as their way out?

Because of this "dream" missionaries often find themselves in rather difficult situations. Many locals think, "Well if these foreign tourists give us what we want, then why don't missionaries do the same?" To them, because we are foreigners, we are able to – and should – give them anything they desire!

This affects our relationships with the people we have come to serve. Our good standing with them seems contingent on what material goods we can provide them with. If we have something to give them, our relationships remain strong; if we don't, relationships quickly fizzle. This is a common quandary for all the missionaries here. Consequently, many of us struggle with the question, "Should we give or not?" Many of the local people are willing to say they are Christians and help missionaries as long as they can benefit from the missionaries. But if they feel there is nothing to gain personally, they don't give missionaries the time of day. This explains why Seib, who lived with us during one term, disappeared once we left for furlough. There was no one to take care of him now. In other words, he had needed Jesus because that kept him connected to us, his source of income to cover tuition and other basic physical needs.

Among the missionaries, there are two main opinions on this matter. Some say we cannot make genuine disciples while giving people material things. However, experience has shown that some western mission organizations operating on this premise haven't seen much fruit. This often seems to be the case for those in African or Muslim areas. The second opinion, which comes from other experienced missionaries, including Koreans, is that we must meet physical needs first and then we can share the gospel. This has its pitfalls as well, obviously, and it appears as though there is no right or wrong answer. Many western missionaries have been cynical about the latter approach, seeing it as antiquated or superficial.

Since Korean missionaries tend to follow the second line of thinking, they are often surrounded by many people waiting to receive whatever they can get, whether it is food, clothes, money – anything. Western missionaries look doubtfully upon the Korean missionaries' tendency to give, thinking, "How much more can you give away? Will it ever be enough? And if it isn't, will these people stick around?"

Korean missionaries are goal-oriented and have a tendency to use "blitz" warfare, hoping to get quick results. They believe they can let the gospel powerfully minister as they feed people spiritually and physically at the same time. Is this the best way? I can't say. What I know is that we Korean missionaries must work together with our co-workers from different backgrounds, both in making decisions and in knowing how best to minister once the decisions are made. Learning from each other's mistakes, we can minimize our trial and error rate, especially since Koreans tend to be on the hastier side. When we have different opinions on an issue and we only stick to our own plans, we often offend our western colleagues. We feel irritated when they take a longer time to make decisions and often cannot understand why they feel the need to take so much time to draft a plan. "Just move forward in faith!" we Koreans may say.

Finding a good middle ground will enable all of us to run a more successful ministry, yet this is easier said than done and I am still left with the same question. Which approach should I take? I agree with the missionaries who say, "Material things can build you a crowd but they won't build you a genuine disciple." On the other hand, I am not convinced that telling hungry souls with nothing in their pockets, "Listen, man does not live on bread alone, but on every word that comes from the mouth of God" will fare too well either.

There is so much need here that, once you start giving, it never seems to be enough. Yet, I have never had the right answer when the locals asked me, "Even strangers buy things for us and provide our tuition fees. You missionaries supposedly came here to help us and claim that you love us, but you don't even have the heart to buy a bicycle for us. Where's the love of this God you're always talking about?"

When I saw the crowd of local youth by the seashore, laughing and frolicking about with the white tourists, I had no idea which way I should follow; the line seems so fine. This is the dilemma of a missionary working in a dreadfully poor country, a dilemma for which no one seems to have the exact answer.

21

DOES AIDS REALLY EXIST?

According to historical statistics, more people have been killed by mosquitoes than by war. The World Health Organization (WHO) estimates that the main contributor to the high infant death rate in Africa is the malaria-infested mosquito. More recently, another killer, AIDS, has swept through the continent. The Ministry of Health states that the sky-rocketing number of AIDS carriers throughout Africa will perpetuate this crisis. Unfortunately, these two diseases have caused a significant amount of bitterness among many Africans towards Westerners, making it harder for Western medical agencies to go into these countries and combat these illnesses.

For general background information, malaria begins with the same symptoms as the common cold, making it easy not to take the symptoms seriously in the beginning. As access to health care in Africa is often limited, those who get sick tend to wait until an illness seems life-threatening to seek help. All too often, by the time the symptoms have worsened, the patient has already missed the chance to receive proper medical treatment early enough to prevent death. This is a common phenomenon among children. A child will lie down with a headache or fever and be dead in the next day or two. To make matters worse, malaria is an irresistible force which our bodies have no immune mechanism to fight off permanently. One could get sick with malaria regularly every month because of the infestation of mosquitoes.

The best malaria prevention is to avoid being bitten by mosquitoes, which is almost impossible. Preventative medications for malaria are not cheap and besides, many people do not take the concept of preventative medicine seriously. Most seem to have an easier time understanding medication as a solution to a sickness rather than as prevention when a person is not even sick. In the meantime, the WHO has tried for many years to eradicate malaria but has not yet found a way to do so. Most people agree eradication is not possible unless the quality of life in Africa can be dramatically improved.

Despite the efforts of the WHO, many Africans have misunderstandings about malaria and AIDS that counter much of the forward movement of medical personnel. Even where I lived, the young people I worked with (even those considered relatively well-educated) often questioned me about foreigners, asking me why malaria was so common in Africa but not in western countries. "How is it that westerners save only their people while so many Africans die?"

It seemed suspicious to them, as if there was a conspiracy of some sort to keep Africa from moving up. I recall one argument a young man brought up, "Do you have malaria in your country? No, right? So if you could beat it in your country which is much bigger than ours, why can't your people do the same thing here for us?" I did not know how to counter this reasoning. Their sense of entitlement and resentment bewildered me and left me with no good answer.

AIDS struck an even more surprising chord. I frequently encountered questions like, "Does AIDS really exist? If it does, how can it be incurable? Is that just in Africa or is it incurable everywhere else in this world?" I was surprised to find that many perceived AIDS to be another disease the whites brought with them to Africa. Some believed AIDS does not even exist, but is merely a scare tactic used by whites to gain power over the birth control of black people. Others believed AIDS does indeed exist, but only whites have the remedy and are refusing to use it for Africans because, again, they want to control the birth rate of Africans. No matter what I said, there did not seem to be a good enough answer to convince them they were wrong. Obviously there was a deeply-rooted sense of victimization caused by foreigners, particularly whites, that had not been pacified generation after generation.

A young lady from Canada came to work in our youth center as a volunteer. One night, she had a conversation with the young folk in the library and discovered that most of them had wrong notions about AIDS. Hoping it was limited to that group of youth, she asked other people at the churches she visited. She was shocked to find most of them felt the same way and came to me greatly disturbed. She couldn't believe how convinced these young people were of their own presumptions about AIDS. How could anyone help these people if met with this antagonism and skepticism towards westerners? I didn't know what to tell this disappointed young lady. She was only one of the millions of people out there who had been totally oblivious to this kind of thinking many Africans possess.

Sadly, this ignorance leads to carelessness and, ultimately, death. Those who do not acknowledge the existence of AIDS do not follow precautionary methods or take preventative medicine of any kind. They live their lives as they desire and if they get sick, that is the will of Allah. What of the babies born with AIDS who have no choice? As these helpless infants die, where does the blame rest? Is it on the ignorance of the parents or, in the end, is it on the devil who would only rejoice at the thought of people dying without having a chance to hear the gospel?

The best way for us missionaries to combat these diseases and the misconceptions is to evangelize, and to do so urgently. When one is transformed by the Holy Spirit he or she becomes a new person in Jesus Christ, striving to live in purity and holiness. Here is genuine Christianity. When we can produce true Christians who change their outlook on life and other people and pursue righteousness, we can help them stay off the deadly path leading to AIDS. As we gain their trust as brothers and sisters in Christ, hopefully we can also take away their misconceptions and distrust of foreigners as well.

22

YOHANA

Yohana, an older bachelor, was our gardener as well as the night guard at our youth center. He was a good man who gave a good impression to everyone. He accepted Jesus and came to church regularly. He had lost his job when his company had to reduce their personnel, so I took pity on him and hired him at the center. His role as a night guard was really just to sleep in the room next to the gate.

I felt it would be good for him to marry. He had a job so he could at least be responsible for a family. I called a meeting and discussed with the local church leaders about his marriage. After some time, the church arranged for him to marry a pastor's relative, and the couple made their new home next to my house. A newly married life literally began.

A few months later, Yohana had diarrhea. I didn't think much of it and gave him some Korean medicine. Usually the local people got well quickly when they took medication, but not Yohana. I gave him all of my medicine, but his diarrhea continued. In fact, he was getting noticeably worse.

I sent him to the public health center nearby and was told he had a hernia, which was the reason his diarrhea persisted. The doctor told me he should have an operation as soon as possible. I rushed to arrange for the operation. Yohana looked healthy for a few days after the operation, but then he started having diarrhea again.

I blamed the doctor for this new diarrhea and asked him for a remedy. Believing it might be from a bacterial infection, he ordered prescription antibiotics. Taking this new advice, I gave Yohana the antibiotics and told him to go home to recuperate. As I visited him in his home, I noticed that he regularly had his Bible on his lap and was reading it. This impressed me and made me think even more that he was an admirable man. I encouraged him in this and earnestly prayed for him, but still he didn't seem to get better.

In the meantime, Yohana became increasingly sensitive and was always quarreling with the five Bible school students in the dormitory. One day he reported to the local pastor that ladies were going into the men's dormitory every night and coming out from it early the next morning. The pastor then came to me and his words hit me like a bolt of lightning. How could such a thing be done by those trustworthy Bible school students whom I loved so much?

I called all of them for an interview and pressed them for an answer. I became upset and told them I would expel them and send them to their hometowns unless they would tell me the truth. They were indignant and denied ever having done the things they were accused of. Then and there, they asked me to go with them to confront Yohana. I believed that such a good man as Yohana would not lie and so agreed to hear what he would say. He told us what I expected.

I shouted at the top of my voice and told the students not to play innocent any more or I would expel them all from the school. Finally, I called a meeting of the school board in order to determine what to do about them. The students couldn't say anything more in their defense and felt they had been hit with incredible misfortune. All of us were appreciative of Yohana who had helped us discover the truth.

Meanwhile, Yohana still had diarrhea. One day I spoke with my close friend, a Japanese doctor, and asked him about Yohana's diarrhea. He was a research fellow sent by the British government to investigate tropical diseases in Africa, particularly to assemble detailed research papers on AIDS. His suggestion shocked me; I was perplexed indeed.

"He might have a fifty percent possibility of AIDS."

I laughed silently. *How could Yohana, who is a good Christian, have such a terrible thing as AIDS? I am absolutely sure that he is not someone who chases women.*

I was confident Yohana's diagnoses would not be AIDS, so he and I went to the Research Department for a blood test. After the test his face went pale and he gasped so much I asked him what was wrong. He told me he was dizzy because the medical doctor had taken so much of his blood. "Who knows," he said, "but that he might take my blood and sell it." He said he would tell our pastor about it and angrily left the Research Department.

I was dumbfounded by what he said and immediately called the doctor and asked him about it. The doctor said he had taken only a moderate amount through a syringe. I was in great turmoil over believing the doctor or Yohana. I did not know which one I could trust. I could not believe that such a good man as Yohana would lie to me. The local pastor did hear about the blood test from Yohana and came to me with a sour face. He also said he was once told that doctors took more blood than was necessary from patients and used it for their laboratory experiments. I regretted that my good intentions were doubted.

Several days later, I went to the Medical Research Department to check the result of Yohana's blood test. The doctor calmly asked to see Yohana instead. I asked him why, and he told me that in general others were not allowed to know confidential patient information. There must have been something fishy when he did not confide in me even though we were close friends. So I no longer asked for the results and took Yohana to him on the following day. Yohana and I went to the main entrance of the Medical Research Department together, but he ran away before seeing the doctor.

As time passed, I discovered that Yohana was a terminal AIDS patient. As a result, he had frequent delusions and spoke out of confusion. The things he had said about the doctor taking too much of his blood as well as about girls coming in and out from the dormitory were all delusion. *Why did he have such a terrible disease?* All of a sudden, I was horrified by the fact that every day our family ate meals prepared by Yohana's wife.

In fact, his wife did not know Yohana had AIDS. In the days before leaving for our second furlough, my family dropped by Yohana's house to have a final family service with him and to encourage him to be ready for his death. He looked like the living dead. He sat down with difficulty, went through the final service, and posed for a photo with my family. He did not admit he was suffering from AIDS and told me he was almost dying due to his serious diarrhea. *What a wretched man he was! What about his wife, Maria? Who could tell but that she would be better off a widow?*

The church sent Yohana to our mission clinic and put him under special care because there was no place else for him to go. He died three weeks after we left for furlough and finally nestled in God's embrace. There was no doubt he had a pure and lovely faith for salvation.

There were more than one hundred chairs made by Yohana in the youth center. He left us, but there were traces of him in every corner of the center. I assumed he had acquired the terrible AIDS virus before becoming a Christian. I could not see his wife after our furlough. I did not know where she was. She would follow after her husband – she would also need to go to the Medical Center some day and would no longer exist on earth like Yohana.

Only a few of the church members knew Yohana died from AIDS. Most of them believed his death was from either serious diarrhea or malaria. They might not have understood how such a good man could die of AIDS. I could not imagine what they would think. Would they distrust the mighty God who could not save Yohana's life? Would many Muslim background believers feel that the same thing would happen to them as a result of their immoral life in the past? Or would they be like Yohana and deny that AIDS exists?

23

ONLY AS STRONG AS MY WEAKNESSES

Some missionary colleagues of mine were working in Bible translation. A young local man named Saki worked with them as a language assistant for two years. Though he wasn't highly educated, he was an astute and organized young man who easily earned the respect of his co-workers. The missionaries whom he worked with shared the gospel with him several times and urged him to go to church but with no success.

One day, out of nowhere, he showed up at the first church I had planted, Alpha Church. Next thing I knew, he was a regular member and even attended Bible study. He would rarely miss a service. A gregarious and eloquent young man, Saki made it easy for the church members to like and respect him. He was especially talented in singing and working with children so eventually I put him in charge of Sunday School. Delighted with his growth, I encouraged him to be baptized but he politely refused and asked me to wait. I figured it was because Saki was subjected to the same harsh familial objections that most of the youth we worked with faced. Family pressure was indeed severe. I understood why he hesitated and didn't push it anymore.

Saki continued to serve in the church and even started to lead one of the cell groups I had started with the church members who lived in his area. There were only four other church members in his group but he led the Bible study with much knowledge and enthusiasm nonetheless. The younger church members and other youth in the village looked up to him and wanted to be like him. He could pray as fluently as a river flows and preach as if he knew the whole Bible by heart. From time to time, I would drop by his Bible study group and observe him leading by candlelight. I would leave thoroughly impressed.

Then a pastor and a deacon I knew from Britain came to visit. We talked about my ministry and I suggested we all go visit the cell groups later that week. They were interested to see what the cell groups here were like. We first stopped by Mojalo's cell group unexpectedly. Mojalo began to get nervous. He stumbled around with his words and struggled with the topics. Saki, on the other hand, did not seemed affected when the three of us walked in and continued cool and collected. He spoke with clarity and conviction and definitely caught the attention of the pastor and the deacon. They were impressed and moved by him and were pleased with the fruit of my ministry. I admit, I couldn't help but feel quite proud of myself that night as well.

To make a long story short, Saki had all of us fooled. An avid Muslim on the inside, he was only pretending to be a devoted Christian the entire time. I discovered the truth later and had no clue why I hadn't been able to see it. Perhaps wishful thinking or pure naïveté – I wish I knew – the bottom line is he had me completely fooled. The day I found out, a young man came running to me exasperated, saying, "I saw Saki praying in the corner of the mosque!"

"You must be mistaken. I don't believe it. It was probably someone that looked like him. Don't worry."

When he kept insisting it was Saki, I admonished him for speaking ill of his brother in Christ and said he should get his facts straight before making such claims. Determined to prove me wrong, he and some others began to look into the matter and found out that Saki was indeed going to mosque to pray every Friday afternoon, interestingly enough right before his cell group Bible study. Still unable to accept this, I decided to go see for myself and there he was, praying in the mosque. No words could express my disappointment. Saki, the young man who was known for his frankness and honesty was kneeling there, praying to another God with such ease that I knew he had never left Islam.

I couldn't understand why he had gone through all the trouble of pretending to be a Christian, leading Sunday school and Bible study. What was his motivation? I wasn't paying him – I had never given him compensation of any kind nor had he ever asked for any! His behavior seemed so outrageous, I would stay up tossing and turning during the nights unable to make sense of it all. It was extremely difficult to see even a single soul saved in this country, and to see Saki in that mosque made me feel like I had lost everything I had worked for.

One evening, I left everything I needed to do and went to Saki's house. I tried to be calm and reason with him, hoping I would understand him more. Once again, however, I had to face the bone-wrenching despair that was all too familiar in the world of mission work. Saki looked at me straight in the eye without flinching and explained why he did what he did. He was charmed by the life of missionaries and wanted to be part of it. His time working with them to translate the Bible expanded his knowledge about the Bible and piqued his interest in Christianity – the novelty of it all drew him in. When he heard about the Alpha church, a church that primarily focused on youth and young adults, it seemed like a perfect opportunity. He was attracted to the dynamics of the church and started to attend. Before he knew it, he had gotten caught up in everything. He proceeded to tell me that he had been and always would be a strong Muslim. He said he could find no difference between Islam and Christianity, except that Islam explained the doctrine of God much better than Christianity did. He believed in the existence of Jesus, but Jesus as a prophet, not God. "How can one equate God and a human like Jesus? Jesus was not God," he firmly stated.

I asked him how he taught Sunday School and led Bible study if he believed these things so strongly. His response truly shocked me. He replied that yes, he had taught about the Bible but never once did he teach that Jesus was the Son of God, and he definitely never compared Jesus to God. I felt such a fool and was so completely discouraged I couldn't find anything to say. Seeing my misery, he continued, "I think it's obvious that I'm not coming to church any more, and even if I did it would never change my faith in Islam." Unwilling to lose Saki, I pleaded with him, "Come on, Saki. Don't be so stubborn. If you keep studying His Word more and pray more, who knows, you may discover the truth!"

There was no convincing him. Of course, I didn't really expect he would take my word for it and give Christianity a second chance.

But I didn't know what else to say. My words felt useless, leaving me feeling small and weak. "Oh Lord, I can't do it anymore. I am only as strong as my weaknesses. Only You can open his heart and take away its darkness," I prayed as I walked away.

We never saw Saki again. One may still find him at the mosque, as strong a Muslim as ever or maybe even stronger. I heard that he is currently a primary school teacher. I don't know what he may teach about Christianity; I'm not sure I want to know. The visitors from Britain often ask about him. Not wanting to think about everything again, I usually resort to a simple phrase the native people here use when they don't know where someone is, "He's around." I sometimes think about how many other "Sakis" are out there working with other missionaries. How many missionaries have taken someone under their wings, someone who seems to play the role of a Christian so perfectly yet his heart speaks the complete opposite? Maybe it is better they don't know. After all, they say ignorance is bliss.

"Not by might nor by power, but by my Spirit" *(Zechariah 4:6)*. *Lord, you alone can transform them.*

24

A FATAL BATTLEFIELD

Ami was a neighbor who often stopped by our house to earn some money by doing housework. Her husband was in Saudi Arabia studying to be a Muslim missionary, leaving her to manage her two children and household alone. Her daughter, Dali, was nine and her son, Ali, was seven. She would always tell them their father was a good man who was devoting his time preparing to do great missionary work for Allah. She and her children took great pride in his Muslim vision.

I don't think I truly understood the depth of the Muslim faith until Ami came around. One day, her daughter Dali was playing around on the parallel bars when we heard her screaming. We all ran outside and saw that Dali had fallen and broken her wrist. It was bent in a horribly wrong way, like a broken tree branch, and I knew she had to go to the doctor right away. I slipped Ami some money to pay for the expensive medical care as she ran off with her howling daughter on her back. It was difficult to see Dali in so much pain, but I knew the clinic nearby would do a good job taking care of her wrist. Besides, she was young and had strong bones that would heal soon, probably within two months.

The following day, Ami came to my house to work as usual. I anxiously inquired about Dali's wrist and she quietly responded that her daughter was under the doctor's care. Judging by Ami's composure, I assumed everything went smoothly and Dali now had a cast on her wrist. To think that was naïve of me. I soon found out Ami hadn't taken Dali to the clinic but to the local witch doctor. Exasperated, I scolded her, "You'd rather have extra money and have your daughter be permanently handicapped? You have to take her to the clinic immediately!" Nodding as if to humor me, she went on with her work smiling calmly which frustrated me even more. As I watched her leave that evening, I was angry with her ignorance – the absurdity of it all!

Four days after the accident, I came home from an afternoon meeting and saw Dali jumping and running around with her friends. How strange, she didn't even have a cast on, just a thin piece of cloth wrapped around her wrist. I ran over to her and examined her wrist. What on earth? There was no swelling or bruising! "How's your wrist feel? Have you gone to the clinic yet?" I asked her. She responded casually that she was still going to the witch doctor for treatment. There must have been some mistake. I called Sarah, a Canadian volunteer who had seen Dali's wrist right when she fell. I wanted to double-check with her to make sure that Dali's wrist had indeed been broken. Sarah couldn't believe her eyes. She vividly recalled seeing the way Dali's hand hung loosely from the point where it broke in a way it shouldn't have. She and I both agreed it was impossible for Dali's arm to look completely healed after four days, even if it had only been badly sprained or dislocated. Unable to make sense of this, I slipped quietly into my house and reassured myself I had been mistaken. It must have been dislocated, maybe it had just looked really bad. Even as I listened to my own voice, I couldn't deny the doubt and weakness I heard.

There was no doubt the devil was at work here. Neither Ami nor Dali believed in Jesus. Ami had taken her to the witch doctor believing that he would heal her daughter's wrist. What did that mean? Could we say that Dali had been healed by the devil?

I remembered how calm Ami had been the day of the accident while the rest of us were hopping around impatiently. It was because she had complete, undoubting faith in the power of the witch doctor and believed in his ability to heal. The work of the devil is vividly real here; his power shown through people like the witch doctor makes mission work seem like an endless uphill battle. When I speak of the miraculous healing power of Jesus, they shrug their shoulders and say, "Why is this guy going on about some invisible man who heals when we have a visible one right here who does the same thing?" To them, Jesus' healing hands are no different from, even inferior to, those of the witch doctor. People here are paralyzed by their fear of the witch doctor's powers; even those who have converted to Christianity are unable to free themselves from the devil's grip. We have baptized brothers and sisters here who still wear charms given to them by a witch doctor when they were babies, fearful of a curse should they ever remove them.

A few years ago, my wife nearly lost her life to a serious disease. When it looked like things were going to turn for the worse, the Lord miraculously healed her, restoring her completely as if she had never been ill. The local people were incredibly excited and informed me the power of Allah had healed her. They said that they had prayed for her, and he had answered their prayers. To me, my wife's recovery was the grace of God. To them, her recovery was the grace of Allah. My confirmation of God's power was their confirmation of Allah's power.

Their faith in their god seemed to mirror my faith in my God, and it was difficult for me to get through to them. As I poured out my testimony wherever I went about this Jesus who heals every kind of disease and pain, they would look at me strangely and wonder why I was boasting as if this were something special. Their witch doctor used Allah's power all the time to heal the sick, they thought. When I said they could be saved if they believed in Jesus, they would simply tell me they had already been saved. When I spoke about redemption, they would say they were already redeemed through their prayers and fasting. When I spoke of eternal life, they would shrug without much enthusiasm and respond, "Yes, Mr. Yoo, we already know. Allah has prepared a place for us to live after we die." What now? Miracles? I already knew that didn't do much. How much more power did they have to witness to see the face of Jesus Christ and not their god? There was nothing I could do by my own words or strength. "Lord, strengthen me so that I do not lose heart at this time. Your power overcomes all things and your love is endless. Fill my weakened heart with your power that changes everyone and with your love so that it overflows from within me."

As I prayed for my discouraged spirit, images of Dali's wrist kept flashing before me. I couldn't help but think about Ami's nonchalance as I scolded her about not caring enough about her daughter to even take her to the clinic. How stupid she must have thought I was for telling her to go to a human doctor who would take months to heal Dali when she knew there was a witch doctor who could heal Dali right away. Had she smirked and thought, "And you think you know better than me," when she saw me examining Dali's wrist in confusion? I felt my pride overcome me, and then the anger began to seep in. "Would she look down upon me now? Have I lost my credibility? Does she think her god is stronger than mine now? Am I overreacting?" Thoughts raced through my mind and I even contemplated asking her not to come to my home any more so I wouldn't have to face her.

The truth is, I shouldn't have lost heart that day over such an insignificant setback. I shouldn't have let my mind succumb to the manipulation of the devil. His oppression is indeed heavy on my shoulders at times, but only because he fears what I can do with the power of God behind me. I am working in a spiritual battlefield. Only two consequences arise from a battle – victory or loss. Losing is out of the question. *Lord help me, grant me the same power and courage that Paul had when he opposed Elymas the sorcerer. Enable me to defeat the devil, not by my might but by the power of the Lord Jesus alone.*

25

THE LURE OF POLYGAMY

I will never forget a young man named Adu. He was very close to my family and was like a younger brother to me. A former Muslim from a coastal tribe, he had known us ever since we planted our first church. He was one of the first local people we befriended when we moved here, and was always so loyal to our family. A handsome fellow with gentlemanly manners, Adu made it almost impossible for anyone to dislike him. He was baptized, and his testimony both overjoyed and broke the hearts of everyone listening. He went on to play a major role in helping us plant another church in a different region. Naturally, the people living there were drawn to him and started coming to the new church. Thanks to him, we saw rapid growth and success in this church. His incredible potential and sincere personality convinced us he would be in our lives for a long time. He was often mentioned in prayer letters I sent out. He was important to me, and I felt personally responsible for his well-being. Whenever I had visitors from abroad, I took them to Adu's home in his village because not only could they see the way the local people lived, but I knew Adu's warm hospitality would make them feel welcome. Adu knew better than anybody how much I cared for him and how much I trusted him.

Adu's family treated us warmly even though they knew we were missionaries. Unlike families of other local people with whom we worked, they didn't care that Adu was so close to our family or served in our church. In fact, they encouraged Adu to be good to us and would even send delicious food with him for us to eat.

One day, Adu's mother went back to her home town in a nearby country to visit relatives. We wished her a safe trip and went about our normal business. Much to our surprise, when she returned she brought a distant family member from her mother's side, a young lady named Aisha. She could speak both her tribal language and Portuguese but not the local language here or English. An attractive, serene girl, Aisha was not yet seventeen years old and was still in high school. She had been betrothed to marry Adu once she finished her studies. Adu was definitely not expecting this and did not feel he was ready to be responsible for a family, so they did not marry but lived together in the same home. However, as one may expect from cohabitation, Aisha became pregnant at the age of seventeen and Adu had to marry her shortly after discovering she was expecting. This type of situation is relatively common here. We were disappointed about the way things happened but moved on.

They had a baby girl named Alma less than a year later. Now a mother, Aisha was kept busy with the baby and all her other domestic duties. She did most of the cooking and laundry for the entire extended family and rarely seemed to have time to rest. I tried to teach Aisha English and the Bible but she simply couldn't commit the time due to her daily demands. Soon, she began to look worn and out of shape, as if she had aged too quickly. Adu was in his twenties, still full of vitality and moving around due to his job. He was always meeting people and spending time outside the home. More importantly, he seemed less interested in spending time with his wife. I felt unsettled as I saw the way Adu looked at his wife; sadly, as though he was tired of looking at her.

One day, Adu came to me, brought up the topic of polygamy, and asked if Christians were allowed more than one wife. I firmly told him that a Christian man should only have one wife, which was the answer he expected although he looked very disappointed by my answer. I told him that he must be a dutiful husband, loving and caring for his only wife, Aisha. He didn't say much and seemed to know what he was supposed to do, so I figured this would be the end of this issue.

I understood where Adu was coming from though. One of his closest friends, Adu's age, had recently taken a second wife who was very young and attractive. Not only that, but Akan, his older brother, also married his second, younger wife in his early thirties. Knowing that polygamy was such a normal, even expected part of the lifestyle surrounding Adu, I wanted to focus on the beauty of having a loyal, monogamous marriage and tried to make my marriage serve as a good role model for Adu and other young people. I hoped they would see the happiness in our Christian family of one man and one wife with their children and want to emulate us. When I taught on this subject of staying loyal to one woman, naturally the young ladies in the church supported me while the young men often protested and questioned me. "Where in the Bible does it talk about one husband and one wife? What about great men like Abraham, Jacob, David, and Solomon? They had more than one wife – Solomon had tons! Having many wives is biblical!" they would argue.

Adu began to join in on the arguments and stubbornly insisted there was nothing wrong with having more than one wife, "No one ever condemned those great men of the Bible for having more than one wife; why is it a big deal now?" As he adamantly attempted to justify polygamy, it was sadly evident to me that Adu had already made up his mind. The more I taught that a marriage under God is meant to include one husband and one wife, the more he pushed for the opposite. We could not convince Adu to abandon his desire for a younger and more attractive wife. I watched quietly as my wife helped Aisha try on different accessories and outfits in hopes of looking more appealing to her husband. I felt sorry for this young girl who still hadn't reached twenty-five and was already being treated like yesterday's newspaper. No woman should ever have to go through this demeaning ordeal.

As long as Adu remained a Christian, he would not be able to pacify his desire for another woman. He knew I would never approve of his taking a second wife because he got tired of his first wife, Aisha. On his left side was the lure of polygamy and on his right was his Christian faith. I knew this would be a difficult battle for him to fight and continuously prayed for Adu, my brother and wingman, desperately hoping he would stay loyal to the Lord and, I admit, to me. He was troubled by his inner struggles and finally came to me one night. Without going into much detail, he told me that he simply had to give up his Christian faith. Without looking at me, he mumbled something about having to stay loyal to his family's religion passed on throughout the generations. What I heard was that he wanted to be able to bring home a second or even third wife if he wished without having his conscience bear down on him. As a Muslim, he would be able to do this without the guilt that would come with his Christian faith.

I quickly dismissed his decision hoping that if he saw my cursory reaction he would think the idea was silly. I prayed my anxiety wouldn't show through. How could he do this to me because of stupid lust? I didn't want the conversation to go any further and sent him home. As I was praying he would beat this, he showed up at my door again hours later. He had been up all night and had made up his mind. He was determined to go through with his decision to go back to Islam. Angry and hurt, I didn't want to listen to what he had to say. As if to encourage me, he told me that all my work had not been in vain. He still believed in Jesus Christ as his Savior and he would never stop believing that. I was completely exasperated, "Listen to what you are saying! Are you serious right now? How dare you stand there and tell me that you believe in Jesus but still want to go back to Islam? And for what?" I yelled. He knew how absurd this was! Most of all, he knew what this would mean for our relationship. As if he hadn't heard a word I said, he started smiling and said, "Mr. Yoo, don't worry. Even though I'm going back to my ancestors' religion, I will also remember the crucifixion."

I was overwhelmed by my frustration, blinding anger, and gut-wrenching hurt. I couldn't hold back my tears. Here was Adu, my most faithful co-worker and closest friend, who was about to turn his back on me and walk away. I held his hands and prayed for him as he shed tears of his own. He knew how much faith, love, and trust I had invested in him. He knew what he was doing would hurt me and leave me feeling betrayed. After my long and heartfelt prayer ended, I asked him one more time, "Are you really going to do this? Adu, my brother, will you really walk away from me right now?" Without a word, he dropped his head in silence and walked out of the room. As I watched Adu disappear into the dark night, I remembered the day he gave his testimony. "I used to live in darkness but now I have found the light and cannot express this joy that I feel!" he had said. The same Adu who had cried as he uttered these words was now returning to the darkness he had once overcome.

How could this be? Of course, I had dealt with this issue before. There had been some believers who had two or three wives they had married before converting to Christianity. They continued to live with all their wives and I had to accept this difficult situation. I could tell them to get rid of all their wives except one. But with Adu, it was different. He had grown up with my teaching from his youth. He had looked up to me and always said he wanted to follow my ways. This made it all the more unthinkable that he had made such a choice. Still unwilling to give up on him, I sent some of his close friends from the church to try and persuade him to change his mind. They returned looking defeated and told me that he was no longer the same Adu, he was so different now. Hearing that made everything worse and I regretted sending his friends. At least I could have clung on to some ignorant hope.

I knew Adu hadn't pretended his faith; I had no doubt that he had met the Lord. He had overcome so many obstacles that challenged his faith. He had suffered a great deal of persecution and ridicule for being a Christian but he hadn't let that shake him. Why couldn't he overcome this poisonous lust for another woman?

After going through this with Adu, I sincerely felt like giving up and going home. I didn't want to trust anybody anymore; no, I couldn't trust anyone anymore. Words can't express the complete despair I felt.

Hadn't this happened enough times already? How many more Adus are out there, how many more times would I have to go through this? It wasn't about differences between religions, it wasn't about cultural differences – it wasn't even about immorality. Ultimately, I was up against the devil and his conniving manipulation and abuse of human nature. Honestly, sometimes I felt like I was losing badly. My back felt as though it was breaking from carrying around all the burdens that come with failure. To me, missions felt like this: you struggle to climb to the top of a treacherous mountain only to find that there is another much higher mountain to climb. Simply put, I was completely burned out.

O Lord, strengthen me. Grant me the calmness You had when Judas Iscariot betrayed You and when Peter denied You. Please restore Adu to Yourself as Peter was restored. I know it is the Spirit who changes man's heart. O Lord, heal my wounded heart first. I desperately need Your comfort and Your power from above. Help me to love these people here despite the deep resentment I feel in my heart.

26

TURNING BACK

"Abu's left, Mr. Yoo."

"Left? Well, where'd he go? When's he coming back?"

"No, Mr. Yoo. He's gone back to Islam."

The day I heard those words I stood there stunned, not sure if I'd heard correctly. Not the Abu I knew! He was one of our most faithful evangelists. Abu had been working tirelessly for his small church in a rural village sparsely populated with people, and a handful of cows and a few donkeys. Abu's dedication to this little church was beyond admirable, and he was truly a blessing to our ministry.

To hear that this man had not only resigned suddenly, but also returned to Islam, which he had sworn was a part of his past, was like a cold slap in the face.

When I first met Abu, he was a struggling blacksmith who had come to know the Lord through some phenomenal female missionaries who had given their lives serving his small tribe. His character was immediately endearing; he was humble, well-mannered, and had a gentle spirit. He successfully completed a string of correspondence theology courses through TEE (Theological Education by Extension). His devotion to the Lord was amazing. His prayers reflected a burning thirst to know Jesus more, his knowledge of the Bible was expansive, and his commitment to the church was one to learn from. This church, consisting of about ten members, was like a family. Located in a strongly Muslim province, the church had been planted by the same missionaries who had mentored Abu. We all greatly appreciated the incredible work of these ladies and most of all, their discipling of Abu.

Abu prayed with more eagerness than anyone else around. When he preached, his exuberance and confidence made anyone passing by stop and listen. He earned much respect not only from the local church members but also from the missionaries. He worked closely with the only ordained pastor in the area and was going to do great things for the people – we thought so anyway. That was why we were all so shocked to discover he had abruptly turned back to Islam.

My mind began to race, trying to understand why Abu would do such a thing. Abu, like most of the other locals, did not know his birthday and was unsure of his age. He guessed he might be in his mid thirties. He had been wanting to find a wife, but this was not easy to do as it was almost impossible to find a young female convert. The local women were under strict cultural restrictions, did not have the liberty to come out to church, and would face severe consequences for turning away from Islam. Consequently, unlike in Korea, most of the members of the churches were men, and most of the women who did come to church were married women following their husbands or were much older. For a Christian man to find a Christian wife in this predominantly Muslim country was extremely difficult. I was aware that Abu had gotten quite anxious about finding a wife so we had attempted to introduce him to the few young Christian women we knew, but none of them seemed to be quite the right match for Abu.

It turned out Abu had fallen in love with a young lady without a husband from his village. She already had two children and lived with her family who were all strong Muslims. He had proposed to her and her family acknowledged his great potential to be a good husband (because he was a recognized leader in his village, ran his own blacksmith shop, and knew foreigners). They applied one condition to their giving him permission to marry their daughter: that he was to give up the Christian faith. Unable to give up his feelings for the young woman, Abu came to the missionaries with this dilemma. Confused and frustrated, he suggested he pretend to be a Muslim so he could marry her and then after they were married, he would be bring her to church. Desperately in love, he thought this sounded like a good idea even though the missionaries and pastor strongly disagreed. To them, he had become like Samson, a man hopelessly disillusioned by his love for Delilah, who easily lured him into her deceitful embrace.

After getting a better understanding of the situation, we were all determined to talk sense into him, hoping we could bring him back. Arguments bounced back and forth between Abu and the church leaders including myself. Finally, unable to handle the pressure, Abu didn't come to worship on Sunday – he went to the mosque to pray instead. Unwilling to accept this, we sent the senior pastor to Abu's house one evening. He pleaded with Abu, rebuked him, and even cajoled Abu all night until five o'clock in the morning. As if he had heard nothing, Abu silently got up and brought in a kettle and after washing his hands, feet, ears, hair, and mouth, he began to pray the heart-wrenching words, "Allah is great. There is no other god except Allah. Mohammed is his messenger." These were the words of the daily incantation resonating throughout the village at the crack of dawn from the nearby mosque, challenging us to awake once again and fight for the Lord – a fight that Abu had once fought so tenaciously. It was truly a painful moment to see the pastor return, defeated and angry; indeed, that was the end of Abu's walk with the Lord. He had returned to Islam.

To add fuel to the fire, we quickly discovered that Abu was beginning to spread defamatory rumors about the mission, even warning people against us and telling them that the only reason we were feigning kindness, providing medical treatment and giving vocational training was a secretive scheme to convert Muslims into Christians.

Of course, everyone in the village knew that our organization was indeed Christian and that we openly shared the Word of God, so this was no surprise. It was more than his public opposition to our mission that hurt us. What Abu had done was speak of the life-long sacrifice and loving devotion of the missionaries in an almost wicked light.

Villagers responded to Abu's return to Islam in different ways. Some joined in Abu's hostility and said, "They can try all they want to convert us, they will only fail. Look at this man who was once the greatest advocate of these people. Even he has realized his stupidity and escaped from their grasp!" Others, however, including the village chief, suspected Abu of being a fickle-minded liar and refused to acknowledge his supposed return to Islam. Even worse, the bride's family was displeased with his lack of integrity and chose not to give Abu their daughter. His entire plan came to nothing.

After I learned of these things, I went to his house early one morning to speak to him.

"Why did you betray us like that, Abu?"

"Mr. Yoo," he started, "it was not betrayal. I was simply returning to the religion of my ancestors after thirteen years of ignorant wandering."

"Then why did you preach, give testimony, and maintain fellowship with us? Was that all just a big lie?

"No, it was a mistake. I didn't know what I was doing and practiced the wrong beliefs."

"Is your heart set on never returning to us then?"

"Yes. I have gone too far to return to you."

"Have you thrown away your Bible, too?"

"Mr. Yoo, there is no reason to throw it away. We believe in the same Allah."

"Where is Jesus now, Abu? Where is the Jesus that you once said confidently was in you?"

"I don't know."

As I got up to leave, I turned to him and said, "Abu, Jesus, the One you believed in for the last thirteen years will never leave you even though you have left Him. Think about all the years you believed in and prayed so earnestly to the God you call the "wrong" one. Those prayers were not said in vain. You are being tempted by something wrong, but the Spirit of truth is calling you back no matter how much you try to shut it out. The further you walk away, the more miserable your life will be. Please, please come back. The sooner you come back, the better your life will be. I don't want you to be another Judas Iscariot who went astray. Please repent and come back, just as Peter did."

He looked straight ahead without making one sound. His heart was hardened, and he wasn't the warm, simple-hearted man I knew. My heart ached so much for him as I took heavy-laden steps towards the door away from this stranger, someone who had worked closely with us for the last thirteen years. I had wanted to know, at least, that he hadn't pretended to be a Christian all those years. Perhaps I was trying to grasp any glimmer of hope; if Abu really had believed in Christ as his Savior, maybe one day he would come back.

I heard a soft voice in my heart as I left that night, "Don't be discouraged, ByungKook. Go and comfort the others. In times like these, that is your job. Remind them of what I promised. 'He who goes out weeping, carrying seed to sow, will return with songs of joy, carrying sheaves with him.' "

All of us did the best we could for Abu. This was as far as our control went. The only thing we could do for him now was to pray for him with love and compassion.

27

A DISCIPLE

One day a man named Mutapo came to see me. He confidently introduced himself as a Muslim teacher who taught history and English in a high school and gave me a favorable first impression. When I asked him the reason for his visit, he coolly responded that he wanted to learn the Bible. I should have been thrilled; if only mission always worked that way. However, I knew why he had really come. I had run into his kind before. I'd had a number of Muslim scholars visit me before Mutapo, asking me difficult questions about the Bible in hopes of trapping or discrediting me. As I was frustrated, I could have responded curtly, but I did not.

I suggested that if he really wanted to learn the Bible, we could indeed set that up. However, this would only be with the condition of setting a regular Bible study schedule during which I would teach him the Word without any interruptions. If he had any questions, they would have to wait until the last day of the Bible studies. If he was interested, I would be willing to start the next day. He thought for a moment as this was probably not the answer he was expecting, but proceeded to agree to the terms and said he'd come the next day after school.

Having learned from my previous experience with hard questions raised by Muslims, I prepared my first Bible study focusing on these very questions. Mutapo showed up the next day as he had promised. I suggested we begin with a word of prayer and started to pray – an earnest, humble but passionate prayer. I don't know if he prayed with me that day or watched me, wondering what made this crazy missionary pray with such emotion. During the Bible study, he quietly listened with no interruptions as agreed. As a matter of fact, he was patient and didn't move during my lengthy two hour lecture and sat silently during the closing prayer. He did the same the next two sessions.

At our fourth session, Mutapo suddenly asked me if he could close the Bible study in prayer this time. Caught off guard, I nodded my head not knowing what words would come out of his mouth. With his forehead glistening with sweat droplets he started slowly and quietly. I will never forget his prayer for the rest of my life. His prayer was one soaked in the honest, hopeful, sincere innocence of a first-time believer. He went on to ask Jesus to be his Lord and Savior. Completely amazed, I think I mumbled what resembled an "Amen." He hadn't asked me any questions so I hadn't had the slightest clue what he was thinking. This man, who had come to me with the intention of breaking me down, before he even got to formulate an incisive question about the Christian religion had become confused and, ultimately, was enraptured by the truth of the Bible.

I gave him my favorite Thompson Commentary Bible which he gratefully accepted and read day and night with an incredible thirst. He even began to teach what he was learning to his class. Knowing Muslims' notions about the Bible, no one was better suited to counter the misconceptions which often led to heated debates with his students during class. He started to teach Muslim history from a Christian viewpoint. His classroom became divided; some accepted what he was teaching and others strongly opposed him, berating him for opposing Islam.

Eventually this news reached the school board which threatened to take away Mutapo's job. He came to see me that night. While I was at a total loss as to what he should do, he was calm and collected and, ironically, reassured me, saying he was prepared for this. If he had to give up his job for Jesus then so be it. Mutapo did lose his job. He became an evangelist, a passionate and fervent one. To anyone who would listen, especially young people, he would share the Word, prepared for refuting any of the questions he had once asked. Many challenged him, but God blessed him with the gift of speaking and no one was successful against him.

As time went on and my friendship with him deepened, I put Mutapo in charge of many church affairs and even personal ones. He became my right hand man on whom I relied more than any other colleague. What a vital member of the church he was and moreover, what an incredible job he did! His thirst for the Word only deepened and his faith in the Lord grew. He went to Haggai Institute in Singapore and completed the course with excellence, achieving the top grade. He often preached at the church and did so with amazing passion and fire, praying for the church and the people with zeal and love.

Some of my colleagues were concerned that I trusted Mustapo too much. They questioned my putting him in charge of many things – what made this local man so special? But I trusted him more than anyone else. I put him in charge of a main building project before I left for furlough, which meant he was to take care of all the related finances – a huge, risky gesture.

When I returned from furlough, much to my disappointment I was informed by my colleagues that Mustapo had managed the finances quite poorly and perhaps I needed to take a further look into things. Upon investigating, I found out that he had taken some of the building money for his own personal use. This upset me, not because I felt a loss over the money, but because it was a complete breach of trust. Did I not put my entire trust in this man? This man who had given up everything for Jesus, why had he betrayed my trust by stealing money?

After that, I inevitably kept Mustapo at a distance. He tried to fix things, but we both knew this was not something to be reversed overnight. He seemed to understand, and from then on we maintained a relationship as acquaintances – pleasant and somewhat shallow. He sought to find his way and recover from his mistake. He began to share the gospel even more; he worked together with another Christian organization newly established in the country and even helped them plant a church. I learned he had made his home the church and people came for services in his house. With his contagious fervor and dedication to the Word, the number attending rapidly grew from ten to over a hundred. I often saw him preaching under the shade of a tree, sweating and gasping with ardor for God as I drove by his neighborhood. I would also hear that wherever he went, he credited me as being his spiritual teacher and even his father. It wasn't easy to drive along as though I was unaffected. I did miss Mustapo and his friendship. At the same time, the sense of betrayal and hurt I felt refused to dissipate and I had no choice but to erase him from my thoughts. My colleagues adamantly reassured me I was making a wise decision by cutting ties with him, and many people questioned him, undermining his credibility as an evangelist. Nevertheless, he continued on as Mutapo, the John the Baptist of the villages. He definitely knew Jesus. That undying commitment he had was one that came only from an intimate and deep relationship with Christ.

Why then did people reject him? Why could I not let it go? Of course, what he had done was wrong. But was it unforgivable? If we were in his shoes, would we have done anything different? Yes, he used the money for himself, but then what about us? As missionaries, do we not use money that's donated for our own purposes so we can live? What exempts locals like Mutapo from using it to live, especially when they have so much less? As I thought of these things, I re-examined my colleagues and myself. Who really is the judge of the legitimacy behind the amount of money I use for my own personal needs compared to how much I use for mission-related work? I began to see myself under the same judgment we used to measure Mutapo and the gravity of his mistake.

Who can say that in the end I am not a bigger thief than Mustapo? Why, my house is bigger than his. My children go to a much more expensive school than his do. As a matter of fact, his children's school barely qualifies as a school. There he is toiling to win one more heart for Jesus in his small corner of the country. Meanwhile, I have purchased expensive airline tickets for our furlough. Which man bears more weight on God's balance?

All the missionaries, even his supposed spiritual father, have rejected this man. Yet he runs and lives for Jesus. If he had not matured in faith by the time I left him, whose fault was that in the end? Perhaps it was his spiritual father's fault, my fault for not training him to be a better man from the beginning, warning him of such temptations. A bad tree cannot bear good fruit – if he is my fruit, then what kind of tree am I?

Today, Mustapo is still fighting hard to spread the truth of the gospel and so am I. The more I think of him and myself, the more I realize the smaller my flame is in comparison to his. How can anyone be a judge of how quickly he lit on fire for Christ? Was it too quickly? "How could a local be so passionate? Does he know enough? Of course that's why he made a mistake" – in the end it all seems like unnecessary chatter. Would it really be an overstatement to say that he has proven to have more passion than most missionaries, is capable of reaching out to more people than we ever could, and that as a matter of fact, he is a man that many of us should be humbled by? Let God be the judge.

28

IS THIS HOW JONAH FELT?

In 1953, a British man and his wife were among the first missionaries to come to this country and work amongst one of the largest tribes. The husband became fatally ill with a tropical disease and passed away within a year. Sadly, the wife eventually had to return to Britain.

The dream of spreading the gospel in this country didn't end, however, and ten years later three European nurses came to this barren land to continue God's work. They opened the first clinic in the middle of a dirt field. This place changed the lives of people living near and far. Being the first hospital to offer desperately needed healthcare, the clinic was known to almost everyone in the country. Making evangelism their main goal, the three nurses dedicated their lives to the hundreds of patients that flocked to the clinic every day.

Lydia, the leader among the three missionaries, was an incredibly strong lady, tougher than a man. Anyone who witnessed how she built the clinic up from nothing in the middle of nowhere could attest to this truth.

One day, she found an abandoned baby left on her doorstep. The infant's mother had probably had this baby out of wedlock and couldn't live with the severe consequences. A missionary's home must have seemed like the only option that would keep her and her baby alive. Lydia took in the child and raised him as her own. She gave him a Christian name and nurtured him into a fine young boy who went to on to complete high school. Lydia loved him deeply and often said this son of hers was the best thing that had happened to her. She trusted him to help her with errands and take care of things for the ministry.

However, as he got older he started to behave strangely and withdrew from Lydia and the other missionaries. He began to steal money from his mother and take part in other inappropriate behavior, causing her great anxiety and many restless nights. He had gone astray, and it seemed there was nothing Lydia could do to bring him back. She had raised him with all the love in her heart, like her own flesh and blood, only to be treated coldly, as if she didn't matter to him at all. As the ultimate betrayal, he left home one day without any warning to look for his biological mother and start a new life. He also left Jesus that day and later became a Muslim. Lydia's hurt was so deep, it eventually caused her to leave the field. She had to go home bearing a painful and unforgettable wound in her heart.

Ten years later, I received a package in the mail from Lydia. She wanted me to pass it on to her beloved son and though I had never met him, I was determined to find him. I had no clue where he lived but fortunately this country is so small it was easy for me to find him. I searched by tracing rumors until I finally discovered where he was living.

I found him at a mosque just having finished his afternoon prayers. He was a handsome, well-built young man, just as I had heard. He was wearing a light green gown over trousers and a pair of clean white shoes. I stared at him for a moment, unable to find the right words to say. I froze as I stood face to face with the one who had broken Lydia's heart. I suddenly felt his mother's pain and understood how deep her wounds must have been. I was sure he didn't understand his mother's heart or know she had never forgotten him and had even sent him this package despite his betrayal.

I fidgeted with the package and hesitated before I handed it over to him. Slowly I managed to start speaking: "Do you remember Lydia, the lady who raised you as her son?"

"Yes, I do."

"Well this is for you, from her, your mother."

He took the package silently and placed his hand on his chest, a Muslim gesture of gratitude. I felt a sense of fear in my heart as he stood there looking away awkwardly. What powerful force had captured and hardened his heart? What is it about Islam that had made this fellow turn away from God and his mother, completely trampling on her love for him? I couldn't leave without saying something.

To just hand him the package and leave didn't seem right or fair. After all the work I put into finding him, to walk away seemed like a waste. "You really have forsaken your mother. But your mother has not forsaken you. God is alive. You once tasted His saving grace and are now standing here today. The farther you go from your mother and from God's love, the more your life will become empty. You must come back soon. his is my advice, your mother's prayer, and God's voice. Otherwise you will fall into ruin." I didn't bother to soften my words because I wanted him to know I meant them.

Despite the stern words from this stranger, he stood there nonchalantly and didn't respond.

I got lost in my thoughts on the way home and found myself thinking, "How could someone like him be chosen by God? Someone capable of such despicable ingratitude – why did God even save his life? Imagine how his mother feels about him, the pain she must feel as she thinks about him and longs for him. And yet, he's probably run home to his new family and is happily opening his package without even the slightest care for his mother." As angry thoughts filled my mind, I felt guilty for thinking this way, but fed up at the same time. I was frustrated – tired of people and how spitefully selfish and cold they can be.

Is this how Jonah felt about the people in Nineveh? I knew this wasn't the right way to think, yet I am only a human myself and quite the hopeless missionary. This is my advice.

29

DON'T BE DISCOURAGED!

There is no mistake about this being a Muslim country. Not only is the president Muslim, but also the vast majority of the population. Muslim law does not govern them, however, and the constitutional law guarantees freedom of religion. There are a number of Catholics and a few evangelicals. The "evangelicals" are those among the A— tribe who heard the gospel through the witness of missionaries and became believers. This tribe are descendants of slaves sold to Great Britain and North America who settled in their original homeland after their liberation. Consequently, they don't live their lives as other Africans because they once lived in the Western world. They don't want to identify with the locals or marry them. They have their own churches, which include both Anglican and Methodist churches which were planted during the colonial period.

"Mission Campaign" was hosted by the missionaries and the A— tribe. We invited a guest speaker from the Billy Graham Association, and both the A— churches and the local African churches prepared for this in prayer during the year. Miraculously, we were allowed to use the square located next to the presidential residence, a kind of playground for the government establishment.

At the same time a large International Islam Meeting was being held. We became tense at the thought of such a meeting occurring during the same period as our mission conference. People were more likely to pay attention to the Islamic meetings rather than our conference, even though our advertising posters were displayed all over the place. In actual fact, all of our posters were torn down within an hour of posting them. When people read them and realized they spoke of a Christian mission conference, they would rip them down. We had to put new posters up again and again. What tedious spiritual warfare! There was no doubt Muslim leaders from neighboring countries were watching us as well.

Finally, the first day of the conference came. The united choir from all the A— and African churches of the nation marched in parade around the capital city. Adults and children alike were intrigued by the loud music and followed us. The square was soon crowded with people, over two thousand by my estimation. The choir sat up front by the pulpit, and hundreds of members of the A— churches sat in the grandstand. Hundreds of Muslim adults and children, men and women were also seated and waited curiously to see what this "performance" would be like.

The choir sang praises, followed by the speaker. He gave a clear simple gospel message and then an altar call.

"Come forward if you want to accept Jesus Christ as your Savior and live a transformed life."

To my surprise, all of the old A— ladies and gentlemen who were seated in the grandstand came forward one by one as if rehearsed. But these were obviously the believers; Christians who had lived their lives within the boundary of churches for years. These "unexpected" people came forward, but so did many of the local children and youth because they were expecting gifts.

The outreach team seemed very excited and filmed the ones coming forward. This was an historic moment – the first open-air outreach meeting in this Muslim country, and they were seeing many converts with their own eyes! The preacher and his team certainly didn't know these were believers from the A— churches, but all of us who had been living in the land knew.

On the second day, once again many people sat in front of the pulpit, but the number of Muslims had remarkably decreased from the day before. In the square there was discord, children being noisy while the preacher was speaking. The preacher gave an altar call once again. The same senior group from the previous day stood up and stepped forward to the pulpit, and the outreach team busily took photos again.

On the third day, at the time to commence, there were no Muslims present, almost as if someone had barred them from entering. We were all embarrassed, but there was nothing we could do. The voice of the preacher became weaker as time came for the altar call once again.

This time he changed his words from, "If there is anyone who wants to accept Jesus as their personal Savior and live a transformed life, then come forward", to "Come forward if you would like to determine to be a better Christian, even though you already have faith in Jesus." Again, the same senior group came forward. Tears came to my eyes, I was touched so much by them. No one asked them to do this, but they did because they deeply respected the preacher and didn't want him to be discouraged. Well, why not feel sorry for him and do such a thing?

On the fourth day, the last day of the gathering, there were no children playing as on previous days: only the preacher, his team, the senior group and volunteers were present. We were no longer embarrassed because the situation demonstrated the spiritual condition of this country. The preacher, too, realized the spiritual reality. Once again, there was an altar call and the same people came forward, but this time no one took photos or filmed.

When the last meeting was over, my church youth put our sound equipment and chairs into the van. We rode home in heavy silence. We were like a sporting team just defeated in a game. Then someone shouted, "Why don't we praise together?"

"In the name of Jesus, in the name of Jesus, we have the victory ..." The van was soon full of song. In a bus traveling next to my van, my Korean co-worker and young folk from another center were all praising Him, too. They must have had the same feeling we had.

My youth raised their voices all the more and praised Him. They didn't care about passers-by who gave them strange looks. This is it! To me, they were my hope. They were Christ's soldiers and the hope for this country, even if their numbers were small. I shouldn't have been discouraged because the response was far fewer then what we have in Korea.

Some knew exactly what was going on and the condition of the nation's Muslims who responded during those four days. Even so, they were not depressed, but singing for victory! They knew what they would have to do in the future and how hard it would be, yet they were praising triumphantly.

We missionaries needn't have felt small. After all, this is a Muslim country, isn't it? What a miracle of grace to see such folk giving praise for the victory by lifting their voices high. And what a miracle that we could finish the gathering without being stoned. How could we not give thanks and praise to Him for that?

30

STOP PRAYING!

I wonder if there is another religion that commands constant prayer as much as Islam. For Muslims, Islam itself is woven throughout their life and culture. It almost seems as though they cannot talk about anything in their life without mentioning their religion. Food, greetings and business are all perfectly, naturally, and harmoniously tied in with Islam. Work can only take up half a day on Fridays because of the prayer time at two in the afternoon. Each person tries to pray five times a day and it is not uncommon to see a driver stop near a mosque at prayer time to have his passengers get out and kneel on the ground in prayer. During this time, businesses don't care about their customers and will shut their doors even if they are busy. The shopkeepers will stand up and kneel down several times while chanting and fingering a string of beads. Regular customers will often wait until prayers are finished, while short-tempered ones go to another shop – but the store owners pay no attention to them.

They have grown up with this prayer life from childhood; this habit of consistent prayer is deeply embedded in their daily routine, almost as though it doesn't require any thought. It's as if the clock says "prayer time" and auto-pray mode sets in – whatever you are doing, stop, drop, and pray. They continue to pray no matter where they are. They will keep their prayer life even in

Christian countries such as the U.S. and Britain and even while traveling. Praying is the most essential part of Muslim life, and their dedication to it is truly admirable.

One day I opened a study center in the middle of the village. On the very first night a dilemma arose. All at once – almost robotically – every student stopped what he was doing, walked over to a neatly cut grassy area next to the study room, and began to pray. I didn't dare stop them as they were all praying so seriously. I stood there, watching them with absolutely no idea what to do or say. Finally, when they concluded their prayers, I walked over and asked them not to pray in the center. "As you all know," I carefully began, "this is a Christian mission center, and I would rather you did not hold your Muslim prayers here." Of course, I knew they wouldn't be okay with my request, but that is all I said. I recalled some students had complained about there being only Christian books in the center and none on Islam. If they had complained about the books, I was sure someone would soon complain about my prohibiting them from praying.

Some time later, a few bold student representatives came to see me. They asked me to make a prayer room for them in a corner of the center so they could pray quietly there. Public prayer places are available everywhere in this country, including inside company buildings and even the airport. Employees stop what they're doing and gather together in these places at exactly five o'clock in the afternoon to pray. Foreign tourists trying to get their luggage may be quite surprised to see this.

I was in trouble. Would it seem contradictory if I didn't allow them to pray when everyone knew the reason I had opened the center was for the benefit of the members of the village, regardless of religion?I firmly refused their request based on the belief that if I conceded to such a demand, they might ask for more. Afterwards, some students began to go home at five o'clock to pray while others came to the center after the prayer time. Though most of them stopped praying in the center, they obviously weren't happy about their loss of freedom to pray. I had to figure out a better way to get them to understand.

One day, walking through the back of our compound, I saw a youth intently praying toward Mecca. My heart sank a little at the sight of this devoted young man with his forehead pressed to the ground. He knew very well he wasn't to pray in the center. I felt discouraged, wondering if I would ever somehow 'beat' the religious zeal of these youth. Rather than staying in the center foregoing the prayer time, students either left, didn't come until after prayer time, or completely disregarded my wishes and insisted on praying. Even within the walls of a mission center, I could not control their dedication to their religion. All I could do was sit there while these people became stronger and stronger Muslims. How could I blame them? They were doing what they knew and if anything, they should be commended for their relentless dedication! If only the church would be more zealous in sending missionaries out into the world to spread the gospel to these lost souls. What could churches and I do to bring all these people to the truth?

I knew I had to do something. I didn't want to give the false impression that we embraced all religions by letting everyone pray to whomever they wanted, but at the same time it seemed a bit harsh to prohibit them from praying, I didn't want them to think all I wanted to do was suppress their religion. A few ideas shuffled through my mind. Would it be easier if I took their names off the library membership list? After all, it was obvious they weren't interested in Christianity. No, that didn't make sense. I would be left with no students in the study center! I was confused and didn't quite know what to do. If I continued to prohibit them from praying, they would think that Christians were narrow-minded and cruel. Would I then have a chance to share the gospel with them? What if I granted their request for a prayer room? That would be bizarre, an Islamic prayer room next door to our church sanctuary! How would that affect the gospel I wanted to preach?

No matter how I went about it, as long as I was controlling their prayer ritual, I would be "that Christian foreigner who doesn't understand." I decided to ask Ali and Kari to handle this matter. They were young men who had converted to Christianity. I remember their first few times attending Bible study: at 5:00 pm they would get up in the middle of discussion and go to the corner to pray. They had been such strong, devout Muslims I wasn't sure how things would turn out with them. Nonetheless, I developed great relationships with both of them. At one point, Ali's father even visited me to see this man he had heard his son talk about. He was the head witch doctor in the village as well as a reputable Muslim leader. I welcomed him into my house and gave him a small gift to let him know I appreciated his visit. He was happy and told me he wished to pray for me. I knew that in their culture it is an insult to refuse another's prayer for you, so I did not know what I was supposed to do. "Do I let him pray to his god for me or do I insult him?" Before I could even respond, he proceeded to pray with complete sincerity, asking his god to bless me. I remember feeling so strange and a bit ridiculous, "Did I just let this man pray to his god to bless me? I don't want any blessings from his god! Did I just lose his respect by letting him pray to his god for me when he knows full well that I am a Christian minister?" What is the best way to stand firm in my faith while not disregarding or disrespecting their religion and offending them?

Would Ali and Kari do a better job at handling this matter? They faced no cultural barriers like I did. There would be no "you versus us" mentality with Ali and Kari. They would appeal more to these students, their friends, if they knew Ali and Kari used to be just like them. Ali and Kari understood where the others were coming from but also knew where I was coming from. I hoped for the best. I hoped that the students would be more willing to listen and understand if they saw the changes in their friends. Some jobs are better left to the experts, I suppose.

PART III

FAMILY

31

QUEEN OF CHILDBEARING

After my wife and I got married, we were excited about starting a family. BoIn got her hands on a book titled *The Queen of Childbearing* and read it all in one day. "I want to be Queen of Childbearing," she would say happily. We had already painted a picture of the perfect family in our minds. Our first child would be a handsome little boy and, a couple years later, a beautiful little girl would follow. When BoIn became pregnant with our first child, both of us hoped we had a little boy on the way. Living in a male-favoring society, Koreans normally want their first-born to be a boy. Of course, when BoIn gave birth to our daughter Jean, we were overwhelmed by how much we loved her and were not the slightest bit envious of others who had baby boys. Right around that time, there was a Healthy Family Planning campaign targeting this preference for boys. "A well-raised girl is much better than ten boys," posters declared. Before long, BoIn was pregnant again and we hoped this time we would get a son since we already had a daughter. I have to admit I was a bit disappointed when our second child was also a girl. But my feeling was only momentary as both our daughters grew up to be healthy and adorable. I could never get enough of them! "If a well-raised girl is better than ten boys, then my two wonderful girls must be better than having twenty sons!" I thought proudly.

Our two little daughters happily followed us to Africa and adjusted very well to their new environment. A few years later, BoIn became pregnant again, a bit of a surprise. We hadn't exactly planned for our third child and were a bit concerned about the baby's health, living in Africa with limited resources. It had been eight years since my wife had had her last baby, and she had recently suffered a great deal from kidney disease and wasn't at her healthiest.

Her third pregnancy was difficult. BoIn. had terrible morning sickness and couldn't eat well. She grew quite weak and I was worried for both my wife's and my baby's health. Two women in our village had recently died during childbirth, which only worsened our anxiety. Even our medical team felt doubtful about my wife having a successful birth here due to her past illnesses and the possibility of her needing specialized care during childbirth which we did not have here. We were a little over a month away from BoIn's due date and decided she couldn't have the baby here. Where could she go? Korea was too far for her to travel. Britain was closer, but there was no place for her to stay before and after the delivery. One evening, while we were praying for this situation, I received an unexpected call from a Korean college friend who was living in New York. He had heard about our situation and had already made all the necessary arrangements for us. A local hospital in New York knew my wife was coming, and family and friends living nearby were ready to care for my wife and child after the birth as I had to stay in Africa with our other children. We are forever grateful to these phenomenal people for doing such a wonderful job of taking care of my wife and baby. Looking back, it is amazing how smoothly everything worked out in such a short time thanks to God's incredible faithfulness.

After a tremendously difficult and painful labor, my wife gave birth to our third child. Meanwhile, I was anxiously waiting to hear from my friend who promised to phone me as soon as BoIn had the baby. He knew how much I wanted a son and was excited that he'd be the first one to get to tell me. The phone rang and I sprinted to the receiver and answered breathlessly, "Hello? Hello? Did she have the baby? How's the baby? Do I have a son?"

"Hi, ByungKook! What's important is BoIn has just had her baby, and both of them are healthy!" he responded, and then there was a moment of awkward silence.

"It's another girl? Really?" I asked quietly. Wait, what was going on? I had been so certain this one would be a boy. BoIn had suffered so much from morning sickness and the baby's aggressive gymnastics routines, it had to be a boy, we thought.

"What's wrong with you, ByungKook? How can you act disappointed? BoIn had a healthy pregnancy in Africa and now you have a beautiful little girl! Be happy, my man! She looks just like you. Maybe you should spend some time praying that she grows up to look like your wife!" he said. I felt weak as I hung up the phone.

Now I had three daughters. "If I have been happy about having two daughters, why couldn't I be happy about having three?" I wondered. I foolishly had gotten lost in my thoughts about what others would think. Culturally, Koreans still placed so much value on boys and I thought about what people would say when they saw me walk by with three girls. "Looks like he was trying for a boy but ended up with three girls," they would say. I was still ignorantly blinded by my antiquated cultural perspective when I should have been worried about how BoIn was managing after going through such painful labor on her own. Whenever I remember that day now, I feel so guilty for thinking those things. I embarrass myself thinking about all those times I stood on my soapbox telling others to "give thanks in all circumstances" when I couldn't even do the same!

We named our new daughter Yevon, which in Korean means "imitate Christ". Bright-eyed and full of energy, Yevon grew up to be an exceptionally bold and happy child. Though she came out looking like me, the older she got, the more she looked like BoIn, which I think everyone could agree is quite fortunate. Everyone says Yevon is the spitting image of her mother, but that's as far as any resemblance goes. I know every parent thinks their child is uniquely special, but I must say Yevon is truly something else. She was the only foreign child in the entire village but she didn't seem to mind. She would invite herself into anyone's house and make herself completely at home as if she lived there. Whenever you saw Yevon pass by, you would see a dozen children flock behind her, most likely waiting to see what other outrageous mischief she'd get herself into. She has been extraordinarily bold and confident since she was a little baby. She would walk up to a complete stranger enjoying a chocolate bar and ask if she could have some. The most surprising act was when she would claim her turn and climb onto the lap of a mother who was nursing her child. Making friends with anyone and everyone has been her gift since she was extremely young. Everyone in the village knew who Yevon was as did all the parents at her school.

When Jean and Lam first left us for advanced education, we were terribly sad and weren't sure we could manage without them. "Life just won't be the same any more," my wife would say teary-eyed. True, life wasn't quite the same, but not because it was miserable. Rather, Yevon's ridiculous antics made us laugh and put us in good spirits. I'm convinced we didn't age as quickly because we had to keep up with her high energy.

BoIn often mentioned that she wanted to have another child. She would watch Yevon playing alone and say, "Honey, it's just not right that she has no siblings here to play with and love. Let's have another one. I haven't gotten rid of the things Yevon used as a baby so we can use them all for the next child!"

"No way! Listen to what you're saying. We could never manage four children. We're not as young as we used to be! Do you know what a huge responsibility another child would be?" I responded as if she had not raised three children already.

When I think about it, perhaps I should have agreed to have another child. BoIn really is the Queen of Childbearing and gave me three amazing daughters who never cease to make me proud. Had we had another one, I have no doubt that child would have been a tremendous joy to us as well.

32

TEARS OVER TOFU

Unlike her first two pregnancies, BoIn suffered from terrible morning sickness during her third. She had no problems during her first pregnancy and never asked for anything which was a true blessing as it was during my seminary studies and we were dreadfully poor. I remember she was perfectly happy eating onions in chili paste. A bit bizarre, but she was content, and this was the same case for the second pregnancy.

The third time she was pregnant we were living on the field, far away from home. Her last pregnancy had been eight years previously, which meant BoIn was quite a bit older this time. She was also having a tremendously difficult time with kidney stones. To make things worse, she craved the most inaccessible foods such as *kimchi* (of course, all the different kinds of *kimchi*, too) and *soondubu*, a stew made from bean curd or tofu. We couldn't buy these things even if we had the money, and I felt sad as she would lick her lips, wistfully longing for tofu. Of all the times she could crave tofu, a food she never really enjoyed back home, she wanted it now. In Africa. Nowhere near a single bit of tofu.

I found BoIn one day sitting on the floor, swollen belly and all, crying. As she rambled on about all the different ways tofu could be prepared, she said all she wanted was a bit of tofu and to go back home. I was fully aware that pregnant women, especially the crying

ones, were not joking when they said they wanted something, and I
wanted to make her happy. I decided to go to a small European
market to see what I could find. To my disbelief I actually found
packaged soybeans and emptied the whole shelf. I knew I could
make tofu with these because I recalled seeing my mother make it
with soybeans when I was a child. I brought them home, excited at
the thought of making tofu, then realized I didn't know how. I
remembered the general process and had seen it a couple of times. I
knew I needed brine but didn't know what exactly it was or where
to get any. I phoned Korea and asked for some brine to be sent by
express parcel. They told me brine is simply saturated salt water
you can get from the ocean. I was in luck as the ocean was less than
thirty minutes away.

Everything seemed to be going smoothly, I had miraculously
found soybeans, we lived by an endless supply of brine – I was
going to make my wife some tofu. I drove to the ocean thinking
about how much I loved BoIn and how happy she would be. I filled
a large bucket with saltwater and brought it home. Now all I needed
to do was soak the soybeans in the brine and grind them with a
hand mill. Hand mill? I wasn't going to be that lucky, but I knew
that a fellow missionary, Sarah, had a blender at her house. "That
would work just fine," I thought blithely as I traipsed over to
Sarah's. BoIn skipped around me like a giddy child around her
mother as she makes her daughter's favorite dish. She couldn't
believe she was actually going to eat tofu in Africa. She usually
enjoyed my unorthodox cooking, typically throwing random
ingredients together, and trusted me to produce tofu.

I had enough ground beans to fill half a bucket. I also had no idea what to do next. Everything was going so well, but now I couldn't remember the next step! I knew you boiled something and squeezed something in cloth but which one came first? Common sense led to me boil the soybeans first, pour them into the cloth, tie it closed with string, and then squeeze the water out. I poured the brine over the boiled soybean paste for the last step. It looked perfect and now all we had to do was wait anxiously for solid curds to form.

An hour passed, then two, and then more. At sunset, the mixture was still liquid. I've never prayed so hard for a liquid in my life. The next morning, nothing had changed. The boiled soybeans never did turn solid. BoIn was so disappointed and I couldn't say a thing, I felt so miserable. It made me feel worse when she pretended not to care and said she didn't feel like tofu anymore anyway. I cried to myself as I poured out the useless soybean juice that was beginning to spoil. The young Gambian folks watched sadly, shaking their heads as this poor man cried over this strange clumpy fluid as he talked to himself. "What does it matter? So what if we can't make tofu? There's other food to eat," I said as I tried desperately to make myself feel better.

I still don't know why the soybeans didn't turn to bean curd. Perhaps something was wrong with either the soybeans or the salt water. I'm convinced the procedure was flawless on my part so it must have been the ingredients. To console BoIn, I promised her that every day on furlough, I would buy her tofu. She said she felt the same as if she had eaten the tofu because she saw how hard I tried. Of course, I knew things would be all right because my wife always found something to eat that made her happy. Our youngest daughter, Yevon, was born healthy and strong without ever knowing how much her mom longed for tofu. It is indeed by God's grace that a baby grows healthily in the womb, not by how much bean curd the mother eats. Yet, to this day I feel sorry I wasn't able to make my wife that tofu.

33

MY THIRD DAUGHTER

Yevon was quite different from her older sisters, Jean and Lam. In many ways, she was like a miniature savage running around in the dirt. As a child, she had a wilder side to her than did her two relatively well-behaved older sisters. For the most part, Jean and Lam were clean and well-mannered young girls who were easy to keep track of. Yevon was definitely a handful – not just a handful of a toddler, but a handful of mud, charcoal, cement, cow manure, or whatever else she was covered in. Typically, like all the other village children, she would spend a lot of time playing outdoors and interacting with the villagers, who absolutely adored her. Sometimes, the outrageous appearance, words, or behavior of our rambunctious, strong-minded little child would shock us so much we did not know how to react to her. I remember a few times when we would look out into the dirt fields and hear her voice but could not actually see her. Older children would always come and take her out to play, and she would come back thoroughly camouflaged in the colors of the earth – out of all the children she managed to become the dirtiest one. She made sure we had our work cut out for us. We would find our two-year-old drinking dirty water that had been used to wash grease-covered dishes at our neighbor's house. She would always be brought home with a piece of chewing gum in her mouth that had apparently made the rounds of all the other children's mouths. I remember the most awkward situation of them all: we went to pick her up in one of the villager's homes and found her suckling the breasts of an older nursing woman. Could anything have prepared us for things like this? I think not. Yevon did not have a care in the world and continued to roam about ever so happily.

When Yevon was a little over three, things began to change as she grew more aware of what was going on around her. We noticed she began to get possessive about the toys, shoes, and other belongings she had. The village children had a tendency to steal her belongings one by one, which she did not like at all. Yevon began to get angry as she saw her toys disappear, leaving her with nothing to play with. All of a sudden, she didn't want to play with the children and even refused to use the local dialects she spoke fluently and would only speak in English. This was a deliberate action on her part not to engage with the local people any more. As she saw the children running off with her toys, she would cry angrily, "I hate these black people!" One day, a girl from a group of young people asked Yevon why she wasn't speaking to them in their language anymore. The response out of this little child's mouth is one I will never forget. She coldly replied, "Why do you ask me to speak your language? I'm not a black girl like you, I'm Korean. Why should I speak in your language? I don't like any of my black friends anymore!" I saw the humiliation in the children's faces, and they were completely speechless. I was so upset and embarrassed with her. I took her home and scolded her severely for saying the things she did. Trying my best to sit a three-year-old down and explain the concept of race and respect, I told her she could not say bad things about her local friends like that and that she was to love them.

Yevon learned her lesson thoroughly and adjusted her language to the best of her three-year-old capability. Whenever her friends ran off with her toys and sometimes her clothes, she would run to me very upset and try to communicate this to me without getting into trouble. She would point to the color of her hair and say, "All right, the people that are this color, I don't really like them but I must love them even though they take my things." I can't help but chuckle when I remember seeing this tiny child struggle so hard to be careful about how to express what she was feeling.

When Yevon turned four, her sisters had to leave this country for further education. This was an extremely difficult time for little Yevon and nothing seemed to console her for a while. We constantly reminded her, "Yevon, you're a big girl now. Like a big girl, you get to eat without help, sleep in your own room, and be brave when you go to school! Remember how Jean and Lam always shared what they had with the local children and how much your sisters loved them? Now these children are counting on you!"

Surprisingly, her attitude about the local people changed completely. She was back to her old self, out roaming around and laughing with them. This time, however, she would take whatever she could find at home like candy, toys, stationery and such, and give it away to her friends and other villagers. She would rummage through the refrigerator for food and cold water and run outside to give it to the beggars that regularly came to our house. Another favorite activity became taking our medical supplies like bandages and ointment and treating her friends who got injured. As you can imagine, we ran out of things pretty quickly. Yevon was beginning to understand the importance of being a "big girl" and sharing with the poor. Whenever we sat down to eat, she would pray so intently for her "poor friends" that she had come to have so much compassion for. She worked hard to make sure everyone around her was taken care of, and those around her felt the sincerity of little Yevon's heart.

Some people got clever and began taking advantage of this. Where we lived, the water system was frequently shut off, so when the water was on we would save water and filter it so that we could drink it. Unlike the locals, we were unable to drink the well water. We would refrigerate our filtered water so we could have cold water to drink in the hot weather. The local people started to get used to having cold water and didn't want to drink the water in the water basins we provided anymore. They knew we kept cold water in the fridge and followed Yevon home. They would ask me for cold water. I would tell them that we were running out of water and they should drink from the well-water basins outside. Of course, I would have loved to have given cold water to everyone that came to my door, but even having a whole fridge full of cold water would not have been enough nor practical. Yevon would then run over and say, "Daddy! We do have cold water in the fridge, silly! There are several bottles of it. I *just* drank some." As she ran over to the kitchen and innocently pulled out a bottle of cold water and poured them generous amounts of it, I couldn't help but feel irritated and scolded her afterwards. Confused, she would exclaim, "But Daddy! Isn't it a lie to say we don't have water when we do?" I did not have a good response.

Later on, we began to worry about Yevon because she was always giving her lunch away and coming home hungry. It was an unnecessary worry, however, because when we thought about what she was doing, she was being a true missionary and loving others according to the Bible. In many ways, she had the purest sacrificial heart, one far better than mine or BoIn's. We had selfishly filled our refrigerator with cold water, but didn't want to share it with others. I had scolded Yevon for being good and doing the right thing while I was not practicing what I preached. I had major forgiveness to seek.

Watching Yevon go about her business, I wanted nothing more than for her to grow up according to His will. That is my greatest prayer. Yevon is a gift given to us from God. How incredible it would be if she grows up to be a phenomenal missionary for the Lord! At such a young age, she's already well on her way.

34

RELIGIOUS FREEDOM FOR YEVON

When my two older daughters first left home, life became boring for their little sister, Yevon, and she lost interest in everything. She would sob and go searching for her sisters. She played with her sisters in her dreams. As time passed, she began to adapt and to get along with local children she once hated. She not only had friends at our center, but also in the village, so she began to go out often. In the beginning, I thought it good that she showed her affection for the other children by handing them candies whenever they came to our house. I let her visit her friends' houses as well. I didn't pay much attention to what Yevon did even though she ate food without washing her hands and drank unfiltered water. Such things didn't affect her because, like the local children, she grew up with them.

What did begin to bother me, however, was when Yevon would put a veil over her head and pray and chant like the Muslims. She even began to memorize the Muslim prayers with her friends. Looking back, I guess this was natural because there were no children apart from Muslims for her to play with and she spent so much time with them. BoIn and I were shocked and scolded her saying, "It's a bad and evil thing to pray to the devil."

One day Yevon saw an entire Muslim family praying and said to them, "My mom said Islam is a bad religion. Your prayers are wrong because you're praying to the devil." Then she tried to pull her friend away from her family. And we found ourselves involved in a small religious war. The family of Yevon's friend flew into a rage and rumors spread quickly. Muslim parents began encouraging their children to tell Yevon that Christianity is the bad religion; that God is in the Koran, not the Bible; that Islam is the real religion. Yevon started to question us openly, "Why do you say Muslim prayers are bad when my friends say they are genuine and good?" We had no idea how to answer her and began to wonder whether something was wrong with our parenting as Christians. Furthermore, she sometimes surprised us with the slang words and lies she used, learned from her Muslim friends who were taught these things from childhood so they were a normal part of their lives.

Because of this, we stopped letting Yevon go out and began giving her Korean lessons by video after school instead. I felt sorry for her when I saw her sleeping at her desk when she was supposed to be studying Korean. Suddenly, we were forcing her to learn Korean, which was like us trying to learn Greek, and she couldn't go out to play as she liked. What agony we were inflicting on our wild horse, Yevon! I regretted not having a fourth child for her to play with.

Yevon's friends didn't understand the situation and would come to our house day and night and call for her to come and play. They couldn't understand her suddenly not showing up in the village. As Yevon talked to them from the window, we felt pity because she looked like a caged monkey. My tenderness won out. I had never been strict with my children so when BoIn went out, I quickly let Yevon escape. Sometimes we would get away with it, but sometimes BoIn found out and when she did, she rebuked Yevon loudly. This in turn would cause an argument between BoIn and me, which added to the confusion and misunderstanding as to why we kept Yevon at home all the time and prohibited her from playing with her friends.

To my tomboy, Yevon, home was like a cell after school. She had to eat unsavory food, learn Korean, and kill time without her friends. When I saw her sleeping a lot and longing after her sisters, I was aware she was getting depressed and becoming too serious. My hope was that as she got older, she would understand us. On the other hand, I also knew these were crucial times for developing her character and was concerned whether we were influencing her for good or for bad.

I often wished I could send Yevon to a country of religious freedom until she grew up. But who could know what other things might await her should she leave us and live elsewhere? As one proverb says, "Out of the frying pan, into the fire." As I thought of such things, I felt sad and wanted to be far away from missionary life. Forgetting what God did for my other two daughters, Jean and Lam, I worried too much about Yevon's future. What little faith I had!

35

THE SINGING CHILD

Ever since she was very young, Yevon has had an extraordinary memory. As a toddler, she would often surprise us by recalling the names of people we had met many months before and the exact location where we had met them. She would pick up the telephone receiver and immediately recognize the person on the other end just by the sound of his or her voice. None of the other children could keep up with her and she seemed quite pleased with herself. I'm not sure how she came to be so bright; she doesn't get it from me. I'm always forgetting something and my wife usually forgets everything. We thank the Lord for this wonderfully exceptional little child.

When Yevon was five, we sent her to a preschool run by an international school. She shared the classroom with a diverse group of children. Two were nationals, one was American, one British, three Lebanese, and the remaining children were from other African countries I cannot recall (of course). Most of the children were Muslim, and her teacher was married to a Muslim man. Yevon was the only Christian in her class.

As I say, she had a great memory and had memorized a large number of songs, whether she knew what she was singing or not. She quickly learned any new song and never failed to be the one singing loudest in the room. She could sing in English, Korean, several tribal languages, and French. She started singing at school, during class and during break time. With her incredibly loud voice, she would sing away without an ounce of embarrassment or consideration for those around her. She would usually sing the Christian songs she had learned. Her favorite songs were "I have decided to follow Jesus" and "Give thanks with a grateful heart." Being the international child she is, she would proceed to sing each song in every language she knew it in. The singing didn't stop. I think the fact that she sang mostly Christian songs didn't help either. Finally her teacher scolded her and told her she was not to sing during school hours any more. Of course, we raised Yevon to be an obedient child. Apparently, she started to hum or whistle the songs to herself.

The Muslim parents of the other children heard about her singing habits but didn't pay too much attention at first. They all found her very entertaining and invited her to their children's birthday parties. I'm sure she did her share (and all the other children's share) of singing there, especially praise songs. Eventually, the invitations stopped coming. How do you deal with situations like these or explain them to a five-year-old? We didn't like the idea of Yevon being left out of everything. At the same time, as missionary parents, how could we tell Yevon to stop singing songs of praise? Finally, we came to a solution. Her teacher had asked her not to sing during school, so we told Yevon to obey. If her friends' parents were going to stop their children from playing with Yevon, there was nothing we could do about that. We would make sure she enjoyed a lot of time with the local children. I suggested she teach some of her favorite songs to the children in the village so they could all sing together. Every opportunity she got she would do this, and soon many of the children and youth that came into the center were singing the songs. Some would even ask, "Who is Jesus?"

One day as I was weeding our garden, I heard Yevon's loud voice singing as usual, "There is none like the Lord Jesus who is holy." Before she finished her song, a youth asked, "Yevon, who is this Lord?" to which she responded, "Who is the Lord? The Lord is Jesus!" He continued to ask her, "Why is he holy?" She spoke confidently, "Because He is the Holy One! Of course He's holy!" I'm sure that didn't quite answer the boy's questions, but it got people talking about Jesus.

Yevon's Muslim friends from the village ended up learning quite a few songs from her and began singing them regularly even though they didn't know what all the words meant. This opened the door for questions and answers about the Lord. I can't say whether little Yevon had a missionary calling or not. What I can say for sure is that our circumstances enabled her to sing as much as she did for Jesus. Had we been living in Korea or in the US, I have no doubt she would have been singing songs she had learned from cartoons, commercials, secular radio and the like. Maybe this is one of the blessings for missionary children.

There isn't much singing in the Muslim world. There's a lot of dancing and drumming, but not many worship songs. In this respect, Yevon helped many of the village members sing. She had them singing songs of praise to the Lord Jesus that they probably will remember into their old age. Yevon continued to sing at school (when she moved up to kindergarten) and in the village. Through her singing, the gospel was being spread.

36

MY BELOVED DAUGHTERS

In our team of missionaries on the field, there are more single ladies than families and no bachelors at all. Perhaps this is because a single man cannot handle living alone in such a place, or because women are more strong-hearted than men! The first missionary to ever come and serve here was a single woman. She was an incredibly phenomenal pioneer who paved the way for many more single women to follow in her footsteps. There are only five families among the thirty to forty members in our team. Other families left after many years of serving here due to their children's education, leaving those of us with younger children behind.

When BoIn and I left Korea with our two young daughters, we gave no real thought to their educational future. We left it up to God and came here. There are only three schools in this country or nearby we could choose from. The first was the missionary children's boarding school in a neighboring country; the second was the Baha'i School and mostly comprised of local children; and the third was an American International School with children from different nationalities.

The first was a good school run specifically for missionary kids (MKs). However, my two daughters were just four and five when we arrived. They were too young to send to a boarding school. We also wanted them to grow up speaking Korean, which they would not be able to do if they went to this school. The school staff advised us to consider their future identity and how being raised in a boarding school might affect them. We were reluctant to send them to the Baha'i school, which had mostly Muslim students. So, despite the expensive tuition, we decided to send our daughters to the International School.

BoIn put her heart and soul into teaching Jean and Lam Korean every spare moment she had. With Korean textbooks scattered on the table, she and my daughters spent many hours reading and writing about Korea and its culture. She was strict about them not using any language other than Korean at home. When she heard them speaking English (which they used in school), she would reprimand them.

Eventually, Jean and Lam were able to use Korean without difficulty which was a tremendous blessing, because for our first furlough in Korea both of them were good enough to attend Korean elementary school. Jean was in fifth grade and Lam was in fourth. They had no problem reading and writing Korean for the most part, but everything else was difficult for them, and they experienced great culture shock. With completely different social and classroom environments and teaching style in Korea, the girls were like fish out of water. Subjects like social and natural sciences were difficult for them to grasp in Korean and the social dynamics among the students were the total opposite from their simple life in Africa.

Rumor quickly spread throughout the school that children from Africa had arrived. Crowds of students came to see Jean and Lam during break time expecting to see black children wearing animal skins. They whispered about the girls' dark skin color and strange clothes. Some students would make animal sounds or mimic Tarzan as my daughters walked by. Coming out of the International School where everyone came from a different country and yet all were close, Jean and Lam were intimidated and hurt by the negative attention they were getting from their peers. They would come home crying and cried every morning before school. They didn't know why they were so hated and why they had to pore over difficult subjects like Chinese and social studies until two or three in the morning. BoIn would stay up with them and, sometimes, the three of them would cry together.

One day, Jean came and knelt down before us. She begged us not to send her to school any more; she cried that she would study all the time and only sleep two hours if that's what it took. She said she was willing to be spanked one hundred times a day if it meant not having to go to school. We hoped both of the girls would soon adapt, but this did not happen and their schooling in Korea ended up being a six-month long nightmare.

When we returned to Africa, Jean and Lam went back to their International School and spent three happy years thriving. Of course, then we encountered the problem that there were no schools to educate them in the higher grades, which meant we would have to send them elsewhere to complete their education. They were adamantly against going back to Korea, terrified of undergoing what they had before but probably worse. We excluded Korea from our options and looked into schools in other places. One in Britain required a tremendous amount of money for tuition, boarding, and miscellaneous costs and seemed out of the question.

We waited anxiously for God's guidance. This time was one of the most challenging and heartbreaking experiences we have ever encountered as missionaries. We felt as though we had brought our children out to the middle of nowhere and would have to watch their future go down the drain. Not only did the thought of sending them away from us break our hearts, but uncertainty about them being alone and vulnerable was downright frightening.

I don't know how many hours we spent praying and crying out to the Lord. "Oh Lord, you have brought us back here to continue our ministry. You know very well about our children's educational future and the heartache it's causing us. Lord, what do we do now? We trust you to take care of this matter, God, but if not, we will take it as your will for us to leave." This was our earnest prayer.

One day I received a very unusual letter from the United States. A Korean couple introduced themselves as a deacon and deaconess who had received God's leading while praying. They believed God had clearly spoken to them that their mission was to look after our children, therefore we should send our two daughters to them. Some of our friends and relatives back home and in other countries had expressed concern for our children and empathized with our struggles. Yet, no one had extended an offer to take on our two teenagers as they knew very well how difficult a job that would be, so this letter did surprise us. We didn't take the offer from this couple too seriously, however, because we didn't even know who they were.

Time passed and we didn't reply to their letter. My colleagues began leaving one by one for the sake of their children's education, and we began to consider this option as well. We felt burdened and worried a lot but continued to pray seriously; that was all we could do.

In the meantime, the couple in the U.S. continued to write us letters, including pictures of their family and home. They strongly believed that looking after our children was their God-given mission. They asked us to trust them, saying they would take care of our daughters and give them the best education. They even sent us a letter from the senior pastor in their church. In the letter, their pastor gave a good recommendation for this couple, commending their faith and personalities.

After much prayer, we were convinced this must be God's answer, took a huge leap of faith, and finally agreed to send our children to them. The couple was overjoyed, and BoIn and I were amazed at God's faithfulness and how He had paid attention to every detail we had wanted for our children and provided every single one. Moved to tears, BoIn and I were brought to our knees in gratitude and praise to the Lord.

He truly lifted what seemed like a hopeless burden off of our shoulders and reminded us that He is in control over everything. I was humbled by His grace and prayed, "Lord, what is man that you are mindful of one like me? Why do you care so much for me? You have taken care of every last detail so my wife and I can continue our unfinished work here. From this day on, I entrust my children and their future and all of my worries into your hands. I will work here with all my heart and strength and do the best I can in this ministry because now I know that you truly want me to be here."

I have an inexpressible amount of gratitude and appreciation for Paul and Kathena Lim and their three children, Haidee, Eunice, and Beau. They changed our lives when they extended their love towards my family and took on our daughters as their own. I thank God every day that this amazing family had the faith and courage to do what they did as I can't imagine all the struggles they went through trying to make room for such a large family physically, emotionally, and spiritually. They took care of my daughters for the next six years until they were old enough to live on their own. Jean and Lam graduated from a good high school and attended the University of Washington, both graduating with Bachelor of Science degrees. The Lims gave my daughters a new life. Without them my daughters would not be where they are today. Our whole family would not be where we are today.

My daughters are now accomplished young ladies who still live in the States. Jean is studying at Johns Hopkins Medical Institute to be a doctor together with her husband, who is also a medical student. My second daughter, Lam, works with families of children with disabilities and is preparing for nursing school. Yevon lives with Lam as she finishes high school. Lam always tells me she now understands so much more all the pains and joys that go into taking care of someone, especially a teenage girl which has its special share of painful and humorous challenges. My daughters still spend time with the Lims and have a great relationship with them. The Lims continue to support other missionary families, changing their lives as well, I'm sure. What a phenomenal couple they are! May God truly, truly bless them for what they have done and continue to do. God is good; His love is enrapturing and His faithfulness is endless.

37

FORGIVE ME, FATHER AND MOTHER

As the third son among my many brothers and sisters, I believe my parents loved me most. This could indeed be a personal delusion, one that all my siblings share in their own minds. Delusion or not, my parents always said, "When we get too old, we want to live with our third son and his family." My father had high hopes for my future success. I had graduated from a good university, married a beautiful wife from the city and had two young daughters. My next step, in my father's eyes, was to find a successful position in a lucrative company and buy a nice home for my new family as well as my parents to live in. When I told him my intention of going to seminary, lines of disappointment became permanently etched into his aging face. He had seen the way local pastors lived; it couldn't have been more antithetical to the life he had dreamed of for his son. "How would we live with you if you're going to be a poor wandering pastor? After all your hard work and success in school, is that the life you want for yourself?" he would ask. Our family was poor, crammed into a small thatched house in the mountains with sometimes no more than tree bark to pacify our hunger. I think my father believed I would be the first to break the chain of poverty that had been perpetuated throughout previous generations. My mother, on the other hand, was an active leader in her church and felt differently. She was very pleased and told me that she would be the most devoted member of my church, praying day in and day out for the success of her son's ministry. Perhaps I could be like the phenomenal pastors in the city she had heard of who built massive churches with thousands of followers.

I hadn't told them of my real goal, which was to become a missionary after graduating from seminary and to leave them and their dreams for my future for the far-off land of Africa. In other people's eyes, I would appear to be the most undutiful son who picked up and left when what I should have been doing was work hard to provide my parents with the life they were not able to have before. That was the role I was expected to play. Instead, I was planning on going to Africa as a missionary, which in my parents' eyes was no different from a death sentence.

Cowering at the thought of telling them the truth, I told them I had to take my family to Britain so I could further my studies overseas (which was true as my wife and I needed to complete the necessary training courses to prepare for mission work). "You have studied non-stop all these years and you're telling us you need to go overseas to study more?" My parents were terribly confused and disappointed, simply unable to find the right words to say to somehow change their son's mind. Despite their futile efforts to convince me to stay, the day of our departure came sooner than I was prepared for. I tried to soak in as much of them as possible as I didn't know when I would see my parents again. They still didn't know that I would be going to Africa after Britain. I wasn't planning on telling them yet, either. I would tell them later, after we had settled in England and I wouldn't have to see their faces. How could I possibly tell them now when I myself didn't know whether I would ever leave Africa alive? They could barely handle the fact that I was leaving for Britain to study. I wasn't about to tell them I was ready to die in a land even further away. The pain I felt in my heart as we walked away from them was one I will never forget, gut-wrenching and suffocating. Nothing could have prepared me for that feeling.

"Anyone who loves his father or mother more than Me is not worthy of Me," played over and over again in my head as we took off for the next chapter of our lives.

We had our first furlough six years after leaving Korea in 1990. My parents anxiously awaited our return, excited to see their son come home as a westernized, sophisticated, Ph.D.-educated man. The expression of utter shock on their starkly pale faces when they first saw us at the airport was one that would make anyone want to run away and hide. Of course, I cannot blame them. After falling seriously ill with malaria a few times, my wife and I had become grotesquely thin and easily looked a decade or two older than we were. To them, my children must have looked like savages that had lived in a charcoal pit all their lives, now pretending to be little Korean girls clothed in faded dresses several fashion trends behind. My mother quietly wept as she ran her fingers over my blackened skin and deep wrinkles. My father looked at my children and cried, "Where have you been and what have you been doing that has made you and your family look like this? *This* is what this place called Africa has done to you? What about your studies – *this* is what you studied for? Why have you aged so much and why do you look like such a beggar? That's enough now, you are at home and we can move on from this." To them, we had completed our missionary work as one completes military service. Drowning in the barrage of questions and sobs, I was too weak to say anything. I knew that we would be going back, but to tell them – where would I begin? They urged and begged me everyday to get involved in pastoral ministry at home. They assured me that there were many places here where we could do whatever ministry we liked and that our experiences from the past would certainly help us in our new work. "Think about it, son. Why go back to that barren land of Africa and sacrifice everything? You really think that you're going to make the slightest bit of difference?"

One Sunday evening, we were asked to make a presentation about our mission work at a church in my hometown, Daegu. We spoke of our experiences as missionaries, the joys and difficulties of living in Africa. We showed a slide presentation of photos we hoped would capture the reality of the people, poverty, innocent lives being lost – we did our best to paint a vivid picture of the land's desperate need for workers. "Do you see how much they are desperate for hope? This is why we must go back, their souls must be saved." I looked to where my parents were sitting and continued, "To save as many souls as we can, we must live with them and serve them for the rest of our days." Now they knew. Now they understood the depth of my commitment to "that barren land" and that the pain of being separated from their beloved son would come once again.

After that Sunday, my parents wanted to spend as much time with my family as possible because they were all too familiar with how much they would miss us when we left. They still tried to persuade us to reconsider working in a ministry at home, that we could serve God *and* take care of them when they got too old. As much as I understood their sincere concern for me, I needed them to understand me and accept that they could not hold me back. I challenged them, "Why do you keep speaking this way? Are you not deacons at your church? Do you only care about lost souls when it doesn't affect you? You are supposed to have faith; where is your faith now?" I was not sure if they understood me, but their despondent faces showed me they now understood that nothing more could be said.

Again, the time to leave came all too quickly, but this time I knew what it would be like when I left them. I wasn't brave enough to do it again. I told my wife that for my parents' sake we should leave quietly without saying goodbye, that they were too old to handle the stress of seeing us leave. The choking pain I felt just thinking about turning away told me clearly enough that my heart might not be able to endure another goodbye – not after the desperation I heard in their voices as they begged me to stay with them. Somehow, they found out our departure date and called us, telling us they wanted to come see us off that day, "This might be the last time we ever see all of you again," they said as I fought back tears. I offered a string of excuses about how the six-hour drive was too far for them, there would be too many people so it would be chaotic, the children would be too sad, the departure time too late or maybe too early...

They didn't argue any further, and we left Korea a few days later. I left without holding my mother in my arms and telling her that I love her. I left my father without telling him that I'd be thinking about him every day. Maybe it's a good thing I didn't; I'm ashamed to say that the day I left them, I left my role as the faithful son behind as well. Consumed in our work, I let their birthdays and important traditional holidays go by forgotten. On these days, a good son would have called his parents and asked about their health and whether they were happy, told them how grateful he was for them, and most of all, asked if there was anything he could do for them. Later I came to know they had missed us dearly every day. They spoke about us any chance they got. Every holiday that passed by, they thought of us and waited by the phone so as to not miss the precious phone call from their son and his family. I wonder how many times they waited before they realized calls were not going to come.

The saying that you don't ever understand the magnitude of your parents' love for you until you become a parent yourself is true. I know I did not understand the pain my parents felt as we left. Maybe if I had known what it feels like to be separated from your children I might not have left. I didn't know what I put them through until the day we had to send Jean and Lam to a far-away country to further their studies. They were still so young and didn't know the first thing about being on their own. As we watched our two beloved daughters walk away, I felt for the first time the unbearable pain nothing can sooth that my parents had felt. Realizing the incredible depth of my own love for my children, I wrote to my parents:

Dear Mother and Father,
Many days and nights have I wept after sending Jean and Lam to
America. Nothing seems to alleviate the pain I feel when I see their empty
desks, unruffled beds, and lonely toys sitting untouched. Words can
never encapsulate how much and how deeply my soul misses them.

When I left you, I thought it would be easy for you to understand my
heart and be quickly comforted knowing that I had gone to work for His
sake. I thought that because your faith is so strong, it would allow you to
let me go. I see so clearly it simply doesn't work that way. I know I'll see
both my daughters around this time next year but it seems like an eternity
– I don't know what I can do to make the time come sooner. No amount
of rationalizing and logic makes watching your children go any easier. To
think we denied you that and left without saying goodbye! How selfish of
me that was! I didn't have the capacity to understand at that time.
Forgive me.

I thought the aching desire to see and hold your children would fade as
time went by. I have not been blessed with such a reprieve. My pain only
seems to get worse and worse like a wound that is reopened each day.
Father, Mother, after sending my children away, I feel your pain and
can't express how sorry I am. How many days have you wept for your son
who is so far away? All the while, I selfishly thought of soothing my own
pain, keeping myself busy so I would not have to think of you both. I am
ashamed. It will be another four years before I see you again. Father,
Mother, your disrespectful, undutiful son cries for your forgiveness under
the African sky. I anxiously await the day when we'll be reunited.

PART IV

MISSIONARY PERILS

38

THE GREATEST NUISANCE

When I was young, I was always told to have pride in the fact that Korea was one of the most homogeneous countries in the world. We had only one race of people with no one of foreign heritage, we all spoke one language, and we all wrote in the same language. To us, this was something special and created a sense of unity among Koreans. As for me, until I entered high school, I had never met a westerner or even anyone who spoke English fluently.

I started to take English classes in middle school. At that point, I did not understand why I had to learn this gibberish that none of us, including the teacher, could pronounce correctly. Our teacher had learned English from another Korean man who had learned English from another Korean man, and so forth. By the time it reached us, it had become a new dialect of English: 'Konglish'. My classmates and I used to joke that if a real Westerner were ever to visit our school, the first person to hide would be our English teacher.

My first exposure to English began with "Good morning." Little did I know that a long grueling battle with English lay ahead of me. Having always been a good student, I began to plow away at my books and lecture notes, memorizing and attempting to embed this English into my head. In middle and high school, I learned vocabulary and grammar. In college, I studied more vocabulary and grammar, and practiced reading comprehension with piles upon piles of books.

After more than thirty years the battle is still going on. I once read a newspaper article that named two countries which experienced the most difficulty in learning English. One of them was Korea. I was not surprised. I am certain much of it is because of the phonetic differences between English and Korean. Of course, most foreign languages are going to be difficult to pronounce, but English seems particularly hard for Koreans. For instance, typically, Koreans use the /l/ sound for the /r/ phoneme, and the /p/ phoneme for the /f/ sound. This applies to many English-speaking Koreans today, including those that have spoken English for many years such as myself. The Korean language does not have words containing either of the two phonemes /r/ and /f/, so our brains have not been tuned to perceive the difference between /r/ versus /l/, or /p/ versus /f/.

I spoke to a fellow missionary whose first language is English about Koreans' pronunciation of English. He mentioned his first few weeks working with another Korean missionary and shared some anecdotes that, fortunately for him, we were both able to laugh about. Every time this Korean missionary had to pray before meals, he would bow his head and say, "let's play" instead of "let's pray," and upon eating, he would say, "good blackfast" instead of "good breakfast". There was also an incident where he was talking about the main ingredient of Korean food, stating proudly that Koreans cannot survive without eating "lice".

A personal experience I had with English was my inability to say the /w/ or the /y/ sounds. My daughter Lam, who majored in

Speech and Hearing Sciences at her university, still tries to help correct my pronunciation, attempting to help me say "wood" instead of "ood", "fire" instead of "pire", "year" instead of "ear". The list of pronunciation errors is long and her attempts usually have the same conclusion – she walks away in frustration.

My youngest daughter Yevon and I stopped by Kentucky Fried Chicken one time while we were visiting the States. Upon ordering some food, I realized that the cashier as well as Yevon appeared to be struggling not to laugh. Apparently, I had asked for an 8-piece kitchen combo. Kitchen, chicken – who on earth thought of the idea to make those two words sound so similar? Although, I wouldn't have minded an 8-piece kitchen for $5.50!

My fellow missionaries and friends from English-speaking cultures give me a hard time about my pronunciation, joking about my less than perfect phonetics. I laugh with them and say, "Brother, you wait until the day we have to learn a language like Chinese or Japanese. I will speak like a native in half the time that you take."

During our years of missionary training in England, we began our first day of English class by introducing ourselves. Next to my wife and me, a young German missionary candidate stood up and introduced himself in terribly broken English with sounds I did not know existed. Even to my untrained ear, his English was extremely poor. With that in mind, I felt better as I was reassured of the fact that there were those who spoke as poorly as me or even worse! However, after a measly three months, this fellow was already having conversations with the teacher and saying eloquent prayers with ease. How is that anything near fair? I studied incredibly hard for countless hours on grammar, pronunciation, and vocabulary.

Most likely, much longer and harder than that German missionary. As a matter of fact, I was being corrected by my two young daughters who followed their parents to England as toddlers and with no special classes or tutoring had become little experts in English. When we moved to Africa, young boys who had barely lived half as many years as I would correct my English or ramble on and on about everything and anything in fluent English!

English – that nuisance! A constant pain in the neck. No, my English skills, or hopeless lack thereof, are what's to blame.

Ever since my wife and I joined WEC, one of the major sources of stress for us has been the meetings. Those countless meetings. Just hearing the word "meeting" aroused stress in my wife and me. The reason was simply English. The meetings were a test of our English skills.. The constant stream of English words that flowed through our ears took continuous sweat and stress to comprehend and retain. Entering the meeting room felt like entering an exam room. We would sit down and prepare for the meeting as if waiting upon a court ruling. On the other hand, next to us sat missionaries who had settled in with knitting or crocheting, nodding their heads as they easily processed what was being discussed, even raising their heads once in a while to voice their opinions or laugh at a funny comment. I always joined in the laughter, but most of the time didn't know what was so funny. At times I completely understood the issues at hand and wanted to voice my concerns. Unfortunately, I wasn't sure how to word them, or if I could relay my message effectively. Usually, after contemplating, I would resort to keeping my mouth shut and letting others make the decisions. Also at times during prayer sessions, I felt convicted by the Holy Spirit and wanted to raise my voice, but I did not trust my English skills enough. To think that in the midst of an earnest, spiritually moving moment I had to worry about something so superficial as language skills was depressing. Others told me I could just pray in Korean, but in a time of community prayer, how meaningful would my prayer be to the others if they could not understand what I was saying? All I wanted to do was freely share and express the prayers flowing from my heart. Even that seemed impossible for me.

We would have visitors from abroad over for dinner, and as my youngest daughter prattled on about what she had learned in kindergarten, they would smile and say, "You speak so well for such a little thing!" They probably said this meaning she was such a bright and intelligent girl considering how young she was. At that time, however, my insecurities would plague me, and it sounded as though they were implying, "Why is it that after all these years, your parents are hopeless when it comes to English? You, on the other hand, at such a young age are fluent and speak English beautifully!" Funny how such a simple phrase became such a complex, personal attack on my pride. That English. Always causing trouble ...

That nuisance of a language was the reason I had to simply paste an awkward smile on my face and pretend I understood what the other person was saying, as my pride would not allow me to ask them to repeat themselves over and over again. That nuisance of a language was the reason I had to pretend to laugh at other people's jokes and respond, "Yes, that's funny," when asked, "Do you get it?" In actuality I had no clue why a chicken crossing the street was so funny, nor did I really understand the point of "knock knock" jokes. I wasn't sure why something like a lettuce would be knocking at the door in the first place. Most of all, that nuisance of a language played cruel games with my pride – during prayer times and during conversations, serious or humorous. English was not my first language. It was barely my second language. I was never going to speak as fluently and eloquently as native speakers, not even close. My pride made that very difficult for me to accept. Thus many times I found myself keeping my mouth closed, keeping my opinions to myself, and letting precious moments of fellowship slip by.

They say the more you know, the more you realize you don't know. This is harshly true. The more I submerge myself in English, the more lost I feel. The more I try to pronounce the words correctly, the more the words become a blend of jumbled sounds. How is it possible to keep studying tirelessly yet fail to achieve your brain's threshold for English? For me, it is apparently possible.

Till this day I wonder whether or not other English speakers understand my broken English and jumbled pronunciation. I find myself chuckling at the thought of "Now, do they really understand me or are they just pretending to spare my ego?" The years I have spent struggling with English are plentiful and so is my doubt. I wonder if my fellow missionaries, native English speakers, understand how much stress and extra effort is involved in learning English? Men and women from Korea, once passionate and vibrant budding missionaries, come abroad to follow their vision only to be discouraged and have their pride harshly depleted by English. Perhaps if English wasn't such a barrier, these missionaries would be able to serve more effectively as active leaders in their team communities. But then, I suppose without English there to humble us, we might walk around unable to get off our high horses in order to focus on serving God in complete humility. Indeed, God finds creative ways to establish humility within His servants.

39

HOW ABOUT THE GIFT OF TONGUES?

The total population of our African land is just over a couple of million. This small country has a hefty share of dialects, which is fortunate because missionaries would have it much too easy if there was only one dialect to master. I would need more than both hands to list all the tribes each of which speaks its own dialect. On top of that, there are many immigrants from neighboring countries who use their own languages from back home. To make things a bit more interesting for the indigenous people, the government decided English would be the main language used in schools because it was impossible to choose one universal dialect out of all the tribal languages. Students are technically not allowed to use their tribal tongue in the classroom but this rule is imposed leniently.

While we were taking our language study course, we had an opportunity to visit a school. We proudly greeted the first teacher we saw on the school grounds in our newly mastered local dialect phrase. Instead of the warm smile we expected, he shot us a cold glare and snapped, "Don't you know that you're only supposed to use English here?" Surprised by his harsh response, we later found out he was actually from another tribe. We were assured that if we had greeted him in his own dialect, his response would have been very different. It turns out, much pride and ownership come with being part of a certain tribe as well as there being an unspoken class system that each tribe falls into. To assume a person is from the wrong tribe is disrespectful, especially if that particular tribe is of lower status than his actual tribe. Probably the elimination of the native dialects in school prevented unnecessary complications.

When we first arrived, we studied hard to master the most common dialect used by many people here. The missionaries who come here generally learn that language first so it only made sense for us to do the same. When we finally decided on our permanent target region, however, we realized the dialect we had worked so hard to learn wasn't going to work there. Initially, we thought because it wasn't too far from the city, we could use the language we had learned, only to discover they used another dialect which we now had to learn. We were back at square one; the language learning process with all its discouragements and challenges was about to start all over again.

Language had already been an obstacle for us. When we left Korea and went to England to prepare for the mission field, our greatest struggle was learning English. Why English must be so dreadfully hard, I can't tell you! Just when we thought we were proficient enough to communicate our basic thoughts, we went to Africa and had to wrestle with the local language for the first two years. Then we had to learn a second dialect. We got our share of ridicule for not being able to speak any of the languages perfectly. I think we can safely say my wife and I faced great challenges. There are some people who only have to speak one language their entire life and go happily to heaven. But of course, we had to learn *three* languages when our aged brains were no longer kind to us. Oh, how I resented the Tower of Babel.

Try to imagine how church services went for us poor missionaries. In a room with fifty or less in the congregation, sometimes four to five dialects were spoken. Attempting to make sure everyone understood what the strange Korean pastor was saying was a weekly challenge. English (in a broken Korean accent) was usually the main language I used and then I needed at least two translators at all times. As expected, my sermons ended up taking a long time, sometimes an hour or an hour and a half. Days when the service would start at nine in the morning and end four and a half hours later I wished my sermons could be, "Jesus is alive! Thank you for coming, see you next Sunday."

Most missionaries who minister under such conditions have a hard time establishing their ground because of the tremendous linguistic barrier. Mastering even one of the tribal dialects is difficult; missionaries have to learn more than one without mixing them up into a stream of meaningless jargon. I was blessed with multilingual ministers in my church – the Bible school students. From different tribes, some of them spoke up to five tribal languages and English on top of that. They knew more than just the greetings in each dialect, too. They were fluent enough to translate my sermons into whatever language was needed. You may be thinking, "Well, the dialects must all be pretty similar if they managed to learn *five*." These dialects are as different as night and day; the only common words are a few derived from Arabic.

Amazingly, these young men had never learned English at school or had any type of tutelage. How had they learned the different dialects and then picked up English? My wife and I had spent years with a personal tutor who taught us the native languages and we still found ourselves sputtering like a dying engine at times. As if I couldn't use a little less trampling of my already defeated ego, those guys had me crying over my pathetic language acquisition skills and even doubting my calling as a missionary. If only all missionaries were blessed with the linguistic absorption of a sponge! Maybe many are, but definitely not this one. And of course, there was my thick Korean countryman accent that added a bizarre staccato-esque rhythm to my already flailing English skills.

I had been learning English since secondary school. I learned more English during my training years in England. Then I learned more while I lived on the mission field for ten years working with multi-national teammates. Yet, till this day, I have yet to become fluent. I think it has something to do with the fact that while I was trying to learn the native dialects, I may have jumbled up my brain's storage of the English language. It seems as though when I learn one language, my brain rids itself of existing language in order to make room for the new one. So, you can imagine what happened when I tried to learn English, and then native dialect number one, and finally dialect number two. It was ugly. I spent a good deal of my missionary life in confusion. I remember many times when I was in a rush or angry, all languages came out simultaneously in a new language of my own. The blank expressions on the local people's faces were truly priceless.

The last straw was when my youngest daughter, who lived on the field from infancy, picked up English and a few of the local languages as easily as if they were abandoned pieces of chocolate.

As she prattled on about her day in one language after another, I turned to God in frustration. What was the matter with me? I remember reading a book written by CT Studd in which he talked about his endless struggle trying to learn Chinese. Exasperated and discouraged, he prayed to God to at least grant him the gift of tongues. I knew *exactly* how he must have felt. "Well, how about just the gift of tongues, then, Lord? Father, have mercy on your servant with a wooden tongue. I have so much I want to say and do, but keep running into the same wall. Lord, help me."

God replied, "ByungKook, it's with your heart you must do My ministry, not with your speech."

"My heart, Lord? Does my heart happen to have the gift of language by any chance?"

Yes, that's the kind of hopeless missionary I am.

40

"PASTOR"

I was ordained as a pastor right before I left for the mission field. Naturally, as expected in Korea, people respectfully addressed me as "Pastor Yoo". Since I had never headed a church as a senior pastor, it was simply a title I had earned after completing seminary. This title later became a stumbling block in my ministry in Africa because, in my mind, certain high expectations came with the title "Pastor" – a typical Korean way of thinking.

When I first moved to the field, no one referred to me as "Pastor". As a matter of fact, no one seemed particularly interested in my title. I couldn't help but be bothered by the fact that after my long and difficult preparation to become a pastor, I wasn't getting the acknowledgement that usually came with the hard-earned status. I was still used to the way things were back home.

I was leading a small service for the local people at that time. I asked the few congregation members to call me Pastor Yoo and most of them did. However, none of my missionary colleagues did, which strangely perturbed me. They were perfectly content with calling me ByungKook, since to refer to their friends and colleagues by their first names was the natural thing for them to do.

Soon the field committee asked me to plant an official church that catered mostly to youth. I started the church based on the way Korean churches worked, which was all I knew at that time because

I had never done any church ministry elsewhere. Church attire must be formal, especially for the pastor, so I put on the best clothes I had. I didn't have a suit so I put on a clean dress shirt and a tie. I put on my best shoes even though my feet were already soaked in sweat from the heat. With my face moistened with sweat, shirt clinging to my back, I headed to the sanctuary for the first service. Everything went smoothly, and the young folks who had come were respectful and seemed to enjoy the service. I'm not sure if it was my formal clothes that made them feel they had to be on their best behavior since they normally saw me in barely any clothes. So far, the Korean style was working, and everyone seemed to get used to the way services went over the next few weeks.

Of course, I reminded everyone to call me Pastor Yoo, not Mr. Yoo. After all, this was church and I was the Pastor, I thought. To my surprise, the title caught on and even people outside of the church were calling me Pastor Yoo. Sometimes, children on the street would run to me and happily greet me, "Hi, Pastor Yoo!" which I thought was endearing. They didn't even know what "Pastor" meant.

Things took a strange turn not too long after that. Some older teenagers and young adults started chuckling to themselves whenever they saw me. "Hey, it's Pastor Yoo," they would say and run off giggling. "Silly kids," I thought, smiling to myself. Most of them were Muslim and weren't familiar with the title "Pastor", so I just figured they thought Pastor Yoo was my name and found it funny. One day, I passed some high school girls on the street. They acted as though they recognized me and asked me, "Are you the Pastor Yoo everyone's talking about?"

They were smiling brightly so I was sure that they must have heard nice things about me. "Why yes, I am Pastor Yoo," I said, quite pleased that non-church people were recognizing me. Suddenly, the six of them burst out laughing, and one of them exclaimed, "You are so funny! Why do you call yourself that?"

Unsure what was so funny, I continued, "Oh I see, you don't know what a pastor is. Well, I am a Christian teacher of the Bible who leads a church. That's what a pastor is."

The laughter started again and another girl responded, "Well, if that's what you want us to call you, Pastor Yoo, see you around!"

I stood there perplexed, wondering what could possibly be so funny. Did Muslims find pastors funny? "Wow, Muslims must really ridicule Christians here. Either that or it must be a teenager thing," I chuckled as I walked home.

Later, I found out they had understood the word "pastor" as "bastard", which was what everyone had been calling me the entire time. Can you imagine? "Hi, Bastard Yoo!" "Good morning, Bastard Yoo!" "Bastard Yoo, I have a question." So now it looked as if I had insisted upon insulting myself and asking everyone to join me in doing so. I had been so concerned about their calling me by the title I thought I deserved that I hadn't even noticed they had been adding a "d" at the end of "pastor".

All made sense now! Those times I had walked through the village and young people had happily greeted me with, "Hello, Pastor Yoo!" I could have sworn it looked as if they were trying not to laugh. Just the other day, I had passed by a group of young men enjoying tea under a tree who had all waved so excitedly, "Pastor Yoo! Have a good day!"

"Now isn't that nice! Look how glad they are to see me," I had said to myself, waving back happily.

I was so set on getting the recognition I thought I was entitled to, that perhaps I did get what I deserved. I had spent so much time making everyone call me Pastor Yoo, there was no way I could go around and reverse everything now. It would be ridiculous to try to correct them all, "No, no, Pastor, not bastard. See, a *pastor* is ..."

Well, this funny "bastard" is still going all over the place keeping himself busy as before. What a shame, I have become the "bastard" and not a messenger of God. As a matter of fact, I had done an excellent job of making God look rather silly with all this "Call me Pastor [bastard] Yoo" nonsense. What was the big deal anyway? Why had I been so worried about a title? Well, what did I expect? Here I was, working in an international setting, yet relying solely on my traditional Korean way of thinking.

41

I MISS YOUR LEADERSHIP

After I had completed all my WEC training, I left my family behind in England while I went on a "spy out trip" to Africa before we moved there permanently. During this trip, one of my main objectives was to meet my prospective field leader. The day I met the field leader, I was shocked to find that out of all the missionaries on our field, our leader was a woman. Having grown up in a male-led society in Korea, I admit I had been certain that in such a difficult field of work, only a man could handle the job of field *leader*. I was also surprised by the appearance of my new field leader. Her dark and firm eyebrows, stern expression and strangely calm yet intimidating air, all led me to draw one stressful conclusion. This field leader was going to be very difficult to please. When she left after our meeting, my pathetic, manly pride attempted reassurance. "She's only a woman. How strong could she be? You're a man. You're the one that should be strong!" Who was I fooling? Obviously Sarah was stronger, and I couldn't help but feel nervous throughout the rest of the trip. The fact that I had never been exposed to a female leader before didn't make things easier. I didn't know what to expect!

Before continuing, let me emphasize that now my relationship with Sarah is one where I feel I can tell her anything and she will always listen with a caring ear. Everything I have said till now about Sarah, I'm sure she will understand and will continue to love us as much as my family loves her.

Back to the middle ages of chauvinistic ideals in which I lived. My family and I arrived in Africa one brutally hot and nerve-racking day. Of all people to meet us at the airport, there she was, that daunting *woman* leader. I again attempted to reassure myself, "She can't be as strong as she looks. Get it together." So began my life as a missionary in Africa.

Sarah, in her job as field leader, paid us frequent visits, offering us all sorts of assistance and guidance. I remember, whenever I saw Sarah's car pull up in front of our house, I had to fight my instinct to hide. Each time, as I expected, she was calm, cool, and quiet. To be honest, in the beginning, my wife and I didn't think we would ever be able to open up to Sarah. However, as time passed we began to get to know, understand and deeply admire her.

During the eight years we worked with Sarah, I wonder if anyone recalls Sarah crying. I vividly remember the day Sarah's beloved mother passed away. Sarah still came to visit us that day. We asked how she was doing and with an amazing calmness she quietly spoke to us about the situation. Listening to her, my wife and I remembered our own parents we had left behind in Korea and our hearts were so heavy, tears welled up in our eyes. Sarah, on the other hand, continued to talk about how much she missed her mother and her sadness about not even being able to attend her mother's funeral due to her current responsibilities and financial limitations as a missionary. That was the only time we ever saw Sarah shed a tear, which would have gone unnoticed if we hadn't been paying close attention. Sarah cried inside.

My wife and I were stunned at the level of self-control Sarah showed us that day. Her maturity and sheer strength made that of my wife and myself seem like tiny specks. Realization of the kind of people we both wanted to be was confirmed that day because of Sarah.

We gave Sarah issues to struggle with. When I first purchased land for the Youth Center and my house, I did so without waiting for the WEC committee to make a final decision about it. Upon finding out, Sarah's only word was, "ByungKook!" Without many words, I could understand everything Sarah was feeling. I knew she was surprised, disappointed, and frustrated at my rash decision, especially now that she had the committee's anger to deal with. Yet with much wisdom she mediated in the situation with astuteness and brought the committee to understand and accept my decision, which was definitely not an easy task. During that time, Sarah taught me what it meant to be part of a team, how to provide the members with appropriate pastoral care, and most importantly, how to effectively lead a team from multi-cultural backgrounds, all simply by her actions. Through watching her, I finally understood the concept of "servant leadership". Here I was, thinking I knew what it took to join an international multi-cultural team because I was an official "member" of WEC, when actually I did not have the slightest clue before meeting Sarah. As a matter of fact, when I first applied to join WEC, I was rejected. Twice. Nevertheless, I did finally become a WEC member, and with the help of good leaders such as Sarah as well as fellow missionaries, I learned about working *together* as a team and how essential fellowship is to the unity of the team. Sarah played a vital role in solidifying the unity of our WEC field team. When she left we saw exactly how important Sarah had been.

Our dear Sarah left our field for Regional Office work abroad. As sad as we were, we accepted the fact that she had to leave. Unfortunately, the empty space remaining in the field when she left was huge. We had been so comfortable around Sarah we didn't even realize what a profound impact she was having on our lives. And then, when she left, we felt her absence in every way. Not that the new leadership was not doing a wonderful job, but even so Sarah was sorely missed. The day I left Africa, I wondered, Will anyone's heart ache over the empty space we leave? Will people say, 'I wish they hadn't left'? Will anyone say, 'What a fine leader he was'?

Without a doubt, Sarah was the furthest thing from what I had judged her to be on the day of our first meeting. She was wise, as were her decisions; her accomplishments were admirable. Most of all, Sarah is indeed strong. It is my belief that God gave her this last name to let people know, the minute they meet her, whom they are up against. Sarah, in my current out-of-the-middle-ages opinion, is actually a leader even *ten* men could not equal.

42

CONFERENCES

Growing up, the one person I feared as much as my father was my schoolteacher. Not only because he frequently scolded me and occasionally used a rod on me, but between my school teacher and me there was an air of authority I could not get past. In Korea, we have a saying, "A student cannot even step in his teacher's shadow," which is the kind of mentality I grew up with during my early years of school.

Things the teacher spoke of in class and wrote on the chalkboard were to be immediately written in our notebooks and memorized, all to be regurgitated on test day. This type of learning went on through middle school, high school, and even college.

Throughout all these years of school, I don't recall a single time when I had a casual conversation, or any conversation for that matter, with my teachers. If there was any type of problem in the school, the teachers addressed it. Students had no say as to which way these problems should be solved. The concept of a student body that discusses issues and works together to solve problems was an unfamiliar experience. This is not the case with schools today. Students create all kinds of clubs and programs, advocating for themselves and their needs.

Yet, despite this change among educational institutions, I believe the Korean church has remained unchanged in many respects. A strict hierarchy exists within the church and there is much less democracy than one would imagine. Much of the time, the voices of the congregation are overruled by those of the elders and the pastor. When the church runs into a problem, the congregation leaves it to the elders to handle everything. Having worked in the church since I was able to work, this is the kind of setting I was used to: teachers run the schools, pastors and elders control the churches.

When my children first started their schooling outside of Korea, teachers would ask to make an appointment for a parent-teacher conference to meet with us to "discuss your child." In Korea, parents were only called for an appointment with the teachers if their children had misbehaved to the point where the teacher's discipline was not enough.

"Discuss? What is there to discuss? All right, what did they do now? It was probably Lam. She must have fallen asleep with the food still in her mouth during lunch time," was the first thought that came to my mind. Lam only did that at home, it turned out. The teachers assured us that Jean and Lam did not do anything wrong at all; they wanted to discuss our children's progress. They wanted input as to what had worked for us and what hadn't in teaching and disciplining Jean and Lam. They also asked for particular concerns we might have concerning Jean and Lam's education. This idea of a parent-teacher meeting was new, odd, and involving.

One cultural difference my wife and I had a very difficult time getting used to when we began working in an international mission was the meetings we had to attend. Once a week, we had a fellowship meeting. Once a month, we had a prayer day. Once a year, we had a field conference. Meeting after meeting after meeting: the meetings themselves were the source of much of my stress. Even though the meetings usually were not in any way unpleasant, the notion of a formal meeting just made me nervous, I suppose. I presume it had to do with the fact that I had grown up in the middle of the mountains, where I had spent the bulk of my time swimming and fishing in the river while gnawing on tree bark. I didn't have to answer to anyone except for my parents and teachers.

In our mission meetings, you had to explain your intentions, reasons, plans, difficulties, and such to those around you. Then you had to listen to their input. Then everyone had to pray for you. There was so much going on in these meetings, so much to remember and consider. Especially the week-long field conferences: from early in the morning to late in the evening, meetings went non-stop. By the end of each night, I would gather up my scattered papers, books, and shattered brain particles, and head back home to rest and recuperate before tackling the next day. If there was one temptation I frequently struggled with, it was the temptation to miss meetings!

Nonetheless, as the number of meetings we sat through increased, I began to appreciate the initially painful scrutiny involved. I saw that for each decision, the thoughts of every member of the field were taken into account, including mine. Realizing that I had a say in all the decisions being made, making suggestions and modifications based on *my* opinions was refreshing. Indeed, this was very different from what I had grown accustomed to at home. Had similar situations occurred in Korea, the final decisions would have been made immediately by the few elected leaders. Even though the whole process now took much longer, each decision involved many individuals of different cultures and perspectives. Because of the time taken to review how each member of the team felt, there were rarely any complaints made by anyone after decisions were made.

Once I began to appreciate these meetings, I had to find a way to enjoy them and perhaps even look forward to them. After living in Africa for a long time, I still found myself becoming slightly anxious about our annual field conference. Perhaps it was because I had to sit on a hard chair all day long. Or perhaps it was because as much as I saw the value and necessity of these meetings, my original upbringing and my nature prevented me from fully adjusting to the western ideal that *"everyone's* opinion matters so *everyone* should get to have a say" practiced in our discussions.

I wondered when the day I would look forward to these important meetings would come. In the beginning I made excuses, convincing myself it was because I was still what they called a "newcomer", so there was plenty of time to adjust. Many years later, I found myself an "old timer" and I still could not get myself to look forward to the meetings. "When will that happen? Is it ever going to happen? Perhaps the day I wake up and find myself turned into a westerner!" I thought.

43

AMONG FAMILY

Out of all my brothers, I loved my youngest brother the most. From his birth, he was attached to my hip and followed me everywhere. That is, until he passed away at a very young age. He didn't go due to an illness or an accident, he took his own life after I left Korea for mission work. I am always tormented by the thought that had I been there for him, I could have stopped this from happening. Until now, no one other than the members of my immediate family knows about my brother's death. In Korea, an incident such as a suicide in the family is looked down upon and thus is kept a deep secret. Moreover, it is assumed that for the brother of a pastor *and* missionary to do such a thing means something must be very wrong with the family.

Amongst our missionary team however, the other members did not seem to have any shame when it came to discussing their family's "bad secrets". They spoke openly of their painful personal issues in the way one openly discusses the weather. Some even shared about their own history as drug addicts and alcoholics, as well as about relatives who were still involved in drugs and alcohol and hadn't met the Lord. Drugs, alcohol, divorce, mental illness and other deeply personal issues were spoken of with honesty and courage. Requests for prayer for family members were brought up and prayed for regularly.

Of course, it is not as if the missionaries discussed these matters with anyone and everyone. They shared such things with us because they saw the WEC team as their own family, a family within which honesty and encouragement comes first. Still, my wife and I found it difficult to really open up and share things we had never spoken about with anyone else. A missionary couple we were close with, good friends, confided in us about their marital problems and asked us to pray for them. Yet, once again, my wife and I could not respond with problems of our own and held back. Even though on the outside we seemed like a problem-free family, we too had our own share of troubles.

Ever since I was young, my parents taught me that family issues were not to be discussed with others because they were personal and private. To let others know our family was struggling was to bring shame upon the family's name. "Saving face" was always a top priority for my family. At times, I remember my parents fighting, bickering and yelling at each other one minute and the next minute when our neighbors came, their expressions and tone of voice changed completely as if they had never fought at all. My siblings and I learned to run over to neighbors' homes and invite them to our house when my parents started fighting.

In Africa, my ingrained mentality that personal issues were not for open discussion was turned completely upside down. Now we were submerged among different cultures, different ideals, and different levels of comfort. Living and working with my new mission family members, I watched hidden secrets exposed and painful memories brought back. Relationships were no longer about saving face, but about comforting, supporting, and creating a safe haven for people to bring their imperfections. Only when a person faces and accepts the honest reality of his life can he humbly lay it all before God's feet and let Him handle everything. To this day, I still struggle and am still trying to step outside my comfort zone and toss out this notion of saving face at all costs. My culture and my nature continue to make this difficult, but this wall is one I must break down and overcome.

44

BOTTOMLESS WATER JAR

Our mission organization has worked tirelessly for decades in this country and it is incredible to look back and see how much has been accomplished. Reaching out to the people living in this small corner of the world has become a story rich with the great sacrifice and ingenious pioneer work of truly phenomenal missionaries. Much of the work in our organization is medical as there is a tremendous need for health care here where there is so much poverty and disease. Medical care is provided freely on the premise that it serves as an excellent tool for evangelism through which many people can be reached.

However, the reality of trying to provide medical care to a population with endless needs is extremely time-consuming and discouraging. From time to time, as a mission-minded team, we evaluated what our primary goals were versus our secondary goals. Often times, the medical personnel of our team were discouraged to find that their work occupied so much of their time that they simply had no room for evangelism.

There were only a few doctors and a few dozen nurses running a large clinic packed with more than a thousand patients in a day (especially during the rainy season when tropical diseases trampled through the villages like a stampede). The staff members cared for their patients even when they came for help in the middle of the night. Rather than expressing frustration and exhaustion, the staff members treated the patients with the mind of Christ, offering them a warm smile and kind service so each one felt at home. The staff members were not forced to behave this way. They believed this should be their attitude and practiced it every day.

On the first Thursday of every month, all of our missionaries gathered to pray and discuss current issues. Everyone was there except for the doctor and nurse who remained on duty at the clinic.

One Thursday, one of the missionaries challenged us with a message from Luke 10:38-42. She asked, "Which is more important, Mary's fellowship with Jesus, or Martha's preparations?" We discussed the fact that we had failed to concentrate on the important matters by getting caught up in the secondary work.

Our medical personnel were highly qualified missionaries when it came to evangelism. Those who came for long-term ministry all had a solid theological background on top of their medical studies. They could easily lead Bible classes, but the problem wasn't ever their abilities, rather the lack of time to do so. Constantly overwhelmed with the medical work, most of the medical personnel felt unsatisfied and down-trodden. One of the medical staff began to speak of her experiences and thoughts. As she spoke, it was if she had rattled a quiet beehive and let loose a swarm of bees. Obviously many of the missionaries had been burdened by the same feelings and by the end of her devotional talk, many of the others were in tears.

Under the umbrella of welfare work, I had already planted a church and had seen some visible fruit. The congregation was

growing and we were blessed with wonderful disciples. As I
listened to these medical workers, my heart felt heavy for them.
Our worlds were very different and as much as both worlds came
with many tears and pain, I couldn't begin to imagine how hard it
must have been for them. I prayed, "Lord, at this moment, I
don't have a single thing to say. What can I do for my colleagues?"
As I prayed quietly, my mind was flooded with memories of Laji
and Mar.

I had planted a church in an overpopulated district and worked
with many youth. Two young men who seemed to know a bit about
the Bible came to visit one day. They both lived quite far away but
somehow managed to always be the first ones at church every week.
After a few Sundays passed, I wanted to know more about these
two young fellows. I asked what brought them to our church, when
they became Christians, and which church they had attended in the
past. They said they had never been to church before but had
attended a Bible study when they were in elementary school. One of
our earlier missionaries, Helga, had frequented their school to
teach them Bible stories. Delighted, I asked if she had known them
personally. They said she probably wouldn't know them by name –
there had been so many children. Helga had been a missionary
nurse for twenty-one years before she returned home a few years
previously. If only she knew, Helga had sown the seeds but never
had the privilege of seeing the fruit of her hard work. These two
young men became wonderful Christians and were eventually
baptized.

I talked about these two men, hoping to offer the incredibly
dedicated medical staff some encouragement. I said I understood

that sometimes it seemed as though they were pouring water into a bottomless jar, or trying to nurture a seed that never grows. But what they sowed now would bear fruit later on, perhaps without them ever knowing. In the future, someone like me would reap what they had sown. Even now, at least one third of the members that attended our services and were part of our youth centers were the fruit of the valuable medical workers in the rural districts. I wanted them to be confident that without their work many of us would not have been where we were. What they saw as "behind the scenes" intensive labor was to me an invaluable part of a partnership that included all of us. Without these medical missionaries who dedicated their lives to taking care of people and speaking of Christ every chance they got, my church planting would not have gone the way it did. I found out later it was a great encouragement to many of them to be reminded of our genuine team ministry. Seeing the beauty and harmony amongst such different people who all came together to work as one team was truly a precious moment.

45

THE PEOPLE I MUST LOVE

In this small, peaceful country, the evidence of extreme poverty can be seen everywhere. According to recent statistics, this nation is one of the ten poorest countries in the world. Its infant mortality rate tops that of all other countries.

There are hundreds of patients who come to our clinics every day, many of them children. Many of the little ones arrive barely alive and are in a critical condition by the time our medical staff get to see them. As a result, they often die in the arms of the doctors which is absolutely heartbreaking.

The doctors often ask the parents when the child first started getting sick and why they waited so long to bring them in. Most of the time, the parents explain that one minute the child was happily playing and then the next minute he or she was lying in bed, terribly ill. In the beginning, the doctors and nurses accepted this answer but it got to a point where too many children were coming too late, and they knew they had to look into this further.

With the help of the local nurses, they discovered that parents were taking their children to the witch doctor at the first sign of illness. They would try the remedies he provided and if those didn't work then the parents would take their child to the local clinic. There were many cases when a child was really healed after seeing the witch doctor. This is the reality of the devil at work here.

An inspiring missionary whose testimony I will never forget comes to mind. She was working as an eye nurse in a clinic in a local village. She treated basic problems and also performed cataract surgery. In proportion to the total population here, a surprisingly large number of people are blind. Working with these odds and a serious lack of eye doctors, she found that in many cases, had these people received proper treatment at the first sign of eye disease, they could have retained their sight. Instead, they had gone to see the witch doctor who had used baseless and absurd remedies, such as pouring donkey urine into their eyes, that only exacerbated their deteriorating eyesight. Determined to counter this trend, she would pack her pickup truck with all her supplies and drive out into the different villages, set up a mini-mobile clinic providing eye care and teach the local people about eye disease prevention. Initially, people from the villages responded with curiosity and a welcoming attitude. They crowded around her and showed much interest in what she had to say. As soon as they found out she was a Christian nurse, however, their demeanor changed and they became hostile towards her. To make things worse, a false rumor circulated the villages claiming that if they went to see this white nurse, she would make their eyes go bad. Villagers began to avoid her or ignore her completely when she tried to talk to them.

She became discouraged. I remember how hurt and exhausted she looked during our prayer meetings as she spoke about wanting to pack up everything and go home. She told us about how she had prayed through many tears, "Lord, they do not know why I am here and for whom I endure such hardship. They are rejecting my treatment and Lord, they are rejecting me. Should I just go home?"

The Lord then said to her, "Be humble. Do not expect to make a name for yourself or get any praise for your work. You must be a servant to them."

Deciding to persevere for Christ once again, she came up with a different plan of action. Instead of going to the villages and waiting for people to come to her, she would go door to door, providing eye examinations and treatment. This was the first time anyone had ever done such a thing. Of course, it was incredibly difficult for her as many people coldly turned her away but she was determined and courageous. Her testimony was powerful and brought us all to tears as she shared her experiences. "These people are blinded not just by disease but by their beliefs. Just because of a matter of religion, they refuse the free gift of sight and salvation. But I am prepared to do even worse things for the sake of Christ; this is only the beginning," she said, wiping away her tears.

Satan's grip on the hearts of the people here is strong. He manifests his power through witch doctors and thepervasive influence of Islam that has such a grip on this nation. This religion is deeply embedded in these people's lives and culture – every day of a missionary's life is a spiritual battle, the same battle that this eye nurse set out to fight on her own. Every morning, she loaded up her truck with her equipment and continued to visit each home in different villages. She refused to pay attention to the scathing looks and snide remarks. She responded to animosity with love and kindness. Though the people's eyes are blinded by the dark today, may their eyes and hearts be opened by the love of Christ one day.

46

I THOUGHT YOU WOULD THANK ME

In the past, foreigners were not legally allowed to possess any land in this country. This had been the government's way of protecting the little land left after years of invasions and colonization by foreigners. Some Middle Easterners who had already lived in the country for a long time became citizens, which enabled them to buy land. Relatively wealthy business men, they quickly bought up the best parcels of land. As foreign missionaries, we had a very difficult time acquiring land and the outlook was rather bleak. It was especially tough for me as my ministry was with youth. I wanted to build a church and a youth development facility for them, but I was constantly discouraged because there was simply no land on which I was allowed to build anything.

In the late 1980s, the law changed so foreigners could finally purchase land. Many people jumped at the opportunity and began buying property, although the Middle Eastern landlords took advantage of this situation and prices shot up on the prime land they owned. I felt we needed to make the most of this opportunity and purchase land for the mission, and proposed this at our next team meeting. Many of the team members agreed with me, but before I could even conjure up the thought of buying any, the best parts of every village were taken. In my eagerness, I quickly began to look at whatever land was still available. I fell upon a lone plot of land on the outskirts of the city. It seemed a good investment to buy this property that had much potential for growth in the future. I had never owned property before, but I did know that people back home had earned a lot of money through real estate, some even becoming millionaires overnight. Land purchased at cheap prices even on the outskirts of Seoul rose exponentially in value because of city planning and development. Realistically speaking, the reason I chose this plot of dirt and wild shrubs was not because it was a promising money-making investment. The bottom line was, fiscally, it seemed to be wise idea to have ownership of some land. More than anything, I wanted to develop a spiritual base on which I could plant a church. My team agreed with this vision and also the logic behind owning property, which would give us more freedom for development.

I urged my team to purchase this land while my Western colleagues meticulously surveyed the property and computed the value, the quality of the land, the financial burden it would be, and other important matters. As I grew a bit restless, my fellow missionaries (as with most Westerners) exhibited more patience and caution than many Koreans such as myself. While they scrupulously considered each aspect over and over, the landowner urged us to buy soon; otherwise, he said, he would sell to others. The land covered nearly 10,000 square meters and was valued at US$4,000.

In the end, I made a big decision. The best way to move this process forward would be to simply purchase the land as soon as possible. I didn't want to spend any more time in speculation about all things that could possibly be speculated about. I would take the next step. This was a decision made with the best intentions for God, I told myself. I would purchase this land for the sake of the mission and Christ. I was excited about my decision. I thought it would be something all the team members could cherish and make something of to serve our mission goals and dreams. I purchased the land myself, without the knowledge or consent of my own wife, BoIn.

In the meantime, my team had been moving towards an agreement for finally purchasing the land. Little did they know it was already ours. As I proudly presented the gift of land to my team, and showed our team leader the purchase papers, her face suddenly turned pale. When I saw her reaction, I was shocked and started to panic. She began stuttering, completely at a loss for words, and did not even know what do with the papers in her hands. Suddenly, I realized how my colleagues felt about a supposed team member who had unilaterally made a decision before the team had come to a final consensus. Others gathered around and were also trying to figure out how to cope with the situation. A critical voice rose among the team members and they rebuked my careless and rash behavior. In truth, I had indeed done what I was not supposed to do.

At that moment, I did not realize what I had done and, with poor judgment, grew defensive of my actions. Two things immediately came to my mind. One was, "What on earth is the big deal?" and the other was, "Why do they rebuke me when I did this for the Lord and the *team*? It's not like I did this for some personal or secular investment. How can they bear a grudge against me rather than thank me and applaud my actions?" Simply put, I reacted from my own subjective, self-centered ideas – I believed others would have the same heart as mine, especially since I did it for the Lord. My propensity to be impatient and careless, that has plagued my character since birth, did not help either.

When I returned home that day, my Korean country man temper took over and I started to grumble to myself. "How can they treat me like I have sinned or something? I did this with the best intentions and even donated the land to the whole team! Why did they push me into a corner and scold me for this as if I'm a child?" My mind began to ramble on, justification after justification, so quickly I didn't even focus on the root of the problem. Like a child, all that ran through my head were excuses to transfer the blame from me without really taking time to think about the hurt or troubles I may have caused for other people. At the end of the day, I had forgotten that I was not the only one working in this land. I was part of a team with members from various countries who had all come together with a singular agenda for the Lord. Team members were supposed to put their heads together and come up with the best decisions for the team as a whole. As a result, decisions were to be carefully thought out and agreed upon by "us", and not just me. Thankfully, our wise and thoughtful leader understood me and eventually so did my colleagues.

This is possibly a problem that may occur again among mission teams which include Korean members. Koreans often tend to be very proactive when they see a problem. The initial intention is not to draw attention and recognition to one's self, it's simply perceived in a sense like a mathematical equation. If you have a problem, come up with a solution and take action as soon as you can so you can move on to the next problem. As you can imagine, this trait, which can be both a blessing and a curse, may often interfere with the cooperative cohesion a multicultural team requires.

47

MISUNDERSTANDINGS

A wrong missionary report

Sending regular reports to his or her sending church and prayer partners at home is very important for a missionary, though it might be annoying at times to write them. I believe communicating is a part of missionary ministry. Especially for those whose home churches are far away and who rarely have visitors from home, reports might be the only way to communicate.

I made many mistakes when I wrote reports to churches. During my language learning period, I shared the gospel with young people whenever I had a chance, although I did not know the local culture well. Everyone I met became close to me and politely told me, whenever I shared the gospel with them, that they would believe in Jesus.

Needless to say, I was very excited and thought evangelism in this Muslim country was a piece of cake. Though the people were Muslims, we were open with them about our faith and they easily accepted the gospel. Naturally, I mentioned their names in my reports. People at home were as eager to pray for them as if they were receiving news of a successful war.

As time passed, I realized that more often than not, the locals were only agreeing to accept Christ in an effort be courteous but had no intention of actually doing so. But it was too late, people at home remembered all of the names I had sent them and prayed fervently for the newly saved souls. Night and day, they had prayed for the protection of these young people from the persecution from their family. I was embarrassed by the situation. How would I take back now what I had reported? I grimaced at the thought of writing, "Most of what I have reported to you thus far is wrong. Actually, most of those saved souls I wrote about were never saved at all." How much easier it would have been to just not say anything at all. Since then, even with a growing ministry I find myself hesitant to write about new disciples and have been more careful than ever about the accuracy of my reports.

Exaggeration

Once my family lived in a remote place where there was no electricity, and we had to go far to get drinking water. Naturally, I mentioned these inconveniences of life in my reports. But an exaggerated rumor circulated at home so people believed "the Yoo family is working in a dreary desert without proper water supply and suffering from a hard life over there."

A local prostitute who lived next door to our house was rumored to have suffered and died from AIDS. I spoke about the seriousness of AIDS in Africa and naturally mentioned her in my report. Later on I received a letter, saying, "I heard you are preaching the gospel among the AIDS patients despite the danger of contracting the disease! You'd better take special care." These incidents awakened me to the need to pay special attention to what I said and think twice about what I wrote.

Another Korean missionary once happily reported that he had

produced the first fruit on his field. Later on he was shocked when he found that his story had become exaggerated and was written up in a well-known Christian magazine as follows: *He won the first convert in the history of one hundred and fifty years of missions in that country.* Though he had shared his joy about his first disciple, somewhere along the line the story had been altered ever so slightly but with major implications for those reading it as well as other missionaries working alongside him.

Sometimes, my children shared the gospel with their school friends. The parents learned about this later and protested, "Why has the school allowed students to do evangelism in school?" I was proud of my children and mentioned this in one of my reports, but at home it was also exaggerated and understood like this: "Missionary kids, Jean and Lam, are doing their missionary job under persecution from their Muslim friends and despite their lives being threatened." I had never meant to exaggerate, but this report turned me into a liar.

Naturally, a missionary may write emotionally about the unparalleled difficulties he or she faces during mission work in the field. But I have found that such a report can often lead to misunderstanding as the story will play itself out differently depending the reader's interpretations. Should I then give only objective, brief facts about my ministry? Would my reports then lose their emotional appeal? How would the readers relate to me, or does that even matter? This is my dilemma.

Sometimes, I received "sympathy" letters from various youth from a home church. They wrote about how they had heard about us from their teachers and imagined what our life in Africa was like.

You must be fighting cannibals and elephants. You must be wandering around the jungle with only fruit of the trees to eat, all for the sake of evangelism. How brave you are, living among the danger of fierce lions, scorpions, and poisonous snakes everywhere. We know you are busy saving lives, but please write to us so that we can always pray for you.

The Africa they had imagined was totally different from the Africa I was living in. There were no elephants or cannibals. The lions were safely contained in a wildlife reserve. I was more worried about cockroaches than dangerous scorpions or snakes. I didn't wander a jungle and I had plenty to eat. As poor as most people here are, there are also those who drive luxurious Mercedes. I never found the time to respond to all the letters and explain that actually, life here is not nearly as bad as they fear. If these are the youngsters who may potentially consider mission work in their future, I pray that what I failed to correct did not cause them to rule out a life in Africa.

Unread reports

Whenever I write a report to our supporters, I give special consideration to the content and presentation. The letter needs to be up-to-date and interesting to engage their attention. These letters are sent so ministry partners will pray for the urgent matters I bring before them and stay in touch with the practical and emotional demands of our job. This helps us feel that we are all part of an extended team; my family works on the field and these letter readers are the prayer workers at home.

Though containing requests for personal prayer, the letters need to be sent as copies. If I tried to hand write each one there would never be time for actual mission work. Bearing this in mind, I try to copy my letters in a manner which visually implies a handwritten note by using a blue color ink in the copy machine, and printing on lined paper so that it appears close to a handwritten note. But despite my efforts, it is still a multiple-copy letter, and some people barely glance at mass-produced letters. They regard them as impersonal reports that don't involve them rather than as a letter containing prayer requests for their consideration.

For instance, I wrote of our sorrowful need for emotional support when we had to send our two older daughters away for their education. Later on I discovered many people had not read the letter. They did not know our children were living apart from us, nor did they know in what city the girls were going to school. Clearly recognizing they did not read my tearful report at all left me feeling isolated and without a prayer net.

During one furlough, I discovered that a supporting church did not know we had a third child. I was disappointed in the lack of knowledge about my family and wondered where my report had been all this time. Not wanting to blame this church for lack of interest, I thought that if the report had been written in my own handwriting, the people might have read it. In contrast, when I saw a ministry partner and a church that remembered what I had written, they were special to me because I definitely felt a genuine partnership.

Now I labor over my reports, trying to make them as captivating as possible in hopes that more people will read them. It is important to me that people know truthfully what is going on so that they can pray for the right things. At the same time, I also understand that even though I try my best to write engaging script, there's still no way for me to know if people will actually take the time to read it. I can only hope.

48

LOCAL "PARTNERS"

A missionary usually works together with the locals in many ways. It should be his obligation to work with them rather than simply employing them. The main reason is that he cannot come to this country with a missionary visa. He can stay only on condition that he is doing social work that benefits the people. Consequently, he must employ as many locals as possible to work on some social project. I, for instance, hired a librarian, a manager, a night guard and a gardener at the youth center.

Nevertheless, I had a difficult time with those who came to me every day hoping for a job. Quite a number of young men in my church did not have jobs and were barely surviving. I felt sorry for those I could not employ because there were no jobs available for them. But, I was not well off either and could not employ everyone who came to me. As a result, those who worked for me always felt guilty around those who did not.

The unemployment rate in this country is hardly worth calculating because the streets are filled with the unemployed. It makes more sense to survey the percentage employed.

Many women are hired by foreigners, most as helpers in missionary houses. Usually there is a lot to be done in these houses because the homes are frequented daily by many visitors. The missionary wives cannot manage the housework alone because they are involved in ministries as much as their husbands. I also hired locals for these reasons and because, if I didn't, they would start complaining about me saying, "These foreigners are so stingy that they don't want to give us a job and share their money with us."

However, a foreign visitor might not understand the situation in our particular country, and might question why I would hire house helpers and not live as the locals did. A Korean living in the U.S. visited the Philippines once, saw the same situation and was disappointed. It was natural for him to react like that because he did not understand the situation in the Philippines. But when he told me about his disappointment, I was embarrassed. I also hired local women to do our laundry and clean the house and the youth center study room because we did not have a washing machine and a vacuum cleaner. I assume if this man were to visit us, he would have the same reaction he had in the Philippines.

There is tension between the two ways of thinking. I called in my house helpers. I had intended to dismiss them, but could not bear to do so, not for our sakes but for theirs. One of the helpers was a single mom with two daughters. If I were to dismiss her, she would lose her means of living. The other helper supported her family. I was between two fires, a typical dilemma for a missionary.

I talked to our helpers from my heart and comforted myself with this: "We are not giving you charity money. You are working hard to earn your keep. You can survive through the work I have given to you. As well, you enable us to do our ministry by working for us. In this light, you become my local partners who help my ministry." I decided I didn't care what people elsewhere thought or said.

49

TOO MUCH SUPPORT?

Every missionary has his or her own story about financial support. Korean churches often still have no clue about the realities of financial support; neither do the missionaries being sent out, even when they go to the field. My family went to the field in the early days of Korean missions.

As far as financial support was concerned, there were two groups of Korean missionaries. One group had an oversupply of support. The other had very low support and was relatively unknown in Korean churches.

I am not sure to which group I belonged. If I had to choose, I would say I did not belong to the former. I am sure God knows which one. Even so, I do not mean my family had less financial support than our Western colleagues. It could be dangerous to judge others by my subjective viewpoint and could lead to misunderstanding. Later I was even told, "Yoo's family has more support than they need."

I know a pioneer Korean missionary who challenged me personally and ultimately led me to serve as a missionary. He was born for missions. He worked in the north of Africa in the beginning days of Korean missions. Several churches and individuals supported his family. At times he happened to have a surplus in his account because of unexpected contributions. He could not send the money back to Korea and looked for a solution. In the end, he decided to deposit the extra funds in a Korean bank abroad with the intention of using the savings for future projects on the field.

Unfortunately, news of the balance in his bank account leaked out and led to a serious problem. I don't know whether this information was disclosed through a bank clerk or someone else with a purpose, but the Korean Christian community in that country found out and the information spread among Korean Christians in North America and finally in Korea. The missionary himself knew nothing of this for years.

Not surprisingly, as the rumor spread, the "amount" in the account snowballed and multiplied and caused resentment among supporters. Years later, I attended a Korean mission conference in Chicago and was told the whole story by a pastor. The amount he mentioned was greatly exaggerated. I was shocked and sorry for the missionary. Nevertheless, I heard this senior missionary had laughed loudly without trying to vindicate himself and made little of the rumor when he finally heard it, despite the misunderstanding it had caused. While listening to the pastor's account, I examined myself and thought more seriously of stewardship in finance.

Sad stories like this are of no benefit to either missionaries or supporting churches. People at home need to totally trust the missionary and have a better understanding of life on the mission field. The situation mentioned was not the fault of the missionary on the field. Hopefully it represents a worthwhile lesson for Korean missionaries as they learn from mistakes in Korean missions.

Some missionary candidates graduate from seminary and go out to the field without a missionary calling, thinking that they can live the easy life. However, there are many more missionaries who go out with a definite calling on their lives and are ready to sacrifice and serve despite the hardships. The churches and prayer partners need to know their missionaries, to place their full trust in them, and to support them prayerfully and financially.

I certainly know that the senior missionary spoken of neither dabbled in investment with the extra money nor put it aside for life insurance or an endowment. I can guarantee that he would use the money for new field projects later on, as he said.

But we must not make the same mistake again. We must improve our thinking about missions. Mission finances should go to the necessary projects in missions. We should no longer argue for or against financial support. A bigger project needs more financial support and some of this might be needed later on rather than immediately. It is mere assumption to judge a missionary by the amount of his or her support without considering circumstances and situations.

On the other hand, a missionary who receives an excess in finances often falls into the trap of multi-tasking to use all of the income for ministry. He or she becomes burned out. In this regard, we Korean missionaries humbly need to learn from other mission societies which have gone through the same trial and error before us. Who knows, we could hear something like this: "Why don't Korean missionaries follow in our footsteps? We did the same thing half a century ago?"

50

FELLOW CITIZENS

The country in which I work is a spiritual wilderness. We came all the way from Korea to work for a breakthrough of the gospel. Other Koreans have come to this same far-off country for a different reason. They came because this county is also a commercial wilderness and they are looking for a breakthrough in business.

Koreans, in general, are gold-diggers. As we have traveled, we have seen Korean businessmen all over the world who have gone to earn a little money. During the last ten years, this kind of Korean has come here to start businesses. Most opened either a wholesale clothing shop or a seafood company (mainly imported prawns). None of them succeeded in their undertaking as they tried to be Korean business people without understanding the local culture.

A Korean businessman started a seafood enterprise about the same time that my family arrived on the field. But he went bankrupt and was forced to leave the country with his children under police guard. A fellow Korean missionary wept as he watched this family board a small boat to leave.

Another Korean family opened a photo studio and seemed to manage it well. One day it closed. The main reason for the failure was that they had started their business without sufficient research about the people and culture

Before we left Africa for furlough, two young Korean couples arrived with lofty ambitions to start a business. One of them had been a photographer years before in a photo studio in my hometown. Here they planned to open a discotheque. Of all the possible businesses in the world, I cannot imagine why they chose to start a discotheque in a Muslim country. But it was too late for me to advise them to consider another business, and they weren't interested in any feedback anyway. The most advanced equipment from Korea was already arriving for their business, and I was not in a position to say anything. The other couple had married just a month earlier and came to Africa while still on their honeymoon. In contrast to the first couple, they consulted me on every detail from choosing a good location to construction workers, laborers and building materials. The wife was especially nice to me as a fellow Korean. Later on they came to me and asked me to translate the words of their discotheque flyer into English.

I did not know what to do in this awkward position. My family and I were the only other Koreans in the country at the time. We were bound to these couples by this national brotherly tie, as well as the more specific connection of being from the same hometown as one of them. I did not know how to honorably refuse their requests. It also seemed they would be unlikely to believe my refusal and would continue to ask for help. My team colleagues and I discussed what I should do; they told me that I must say "No" even though the couples were Koreans, because the nature of their business was against what we ourselves were trying to do to influence local behavior.

You might laugh at me, but I had lost my heart to these young couples who were fellow Koreans. Indeed, I forgot my convictions as a missionary because of the strong tie to a far-off land. I had already stopped by their construction site several times to see their efforts. When I saw how hard they were working, without even taking time to eat, my first thought was that Koreans are a great race.

I forgot about the discotheque for a moment and wished that they would succeed in their business. Sometimes, they invited my family to dinner. Then I had to pray for them and it would be rude if I did not also pray that their business would be blessed and that they would enjoy success in the future. I did not want to see them having to leave Africa in tears. You may not understand this sense of needing to be supportive of another Korean even if I didn't like his work. We hardly see our countrymen here. I could well imagine this conflict as I had watched my Japanese friend, who was a Catholic, regularly invite local Japanese Jehovah's Witnesses to dinner at his home just to enjoy the company of a fellow countryman. Our departure from Africa was drawing near and so was the opening day for the discotheque. If the opening ceremony took place before we left, I knew they would invite me to pray at the celebration. What on earth would I do? I am thankful to God that my family left first; the couples' containers were delayed in arriving so the opening was put back.

You might ask how a pastor could wish the success of a discotheque, but I did so from the bottom of my heart. What a contradiction! I usually preached, "Dancing in a discotheque is like dancing in a hellish way." I knew what I believed. But, I really did not want to see these fellow Koreans fail and leave the country in tears. After we left, I heard they wasted their money and left the country less than three months later. Is this country really a wilderness to hurt every Korean except missionaries?

I will go back there. And I will bury my ashes there. I don't know why I love this country so much though those who failed there might be utterly disgusted with it. If the young couples were to read this writing, what would they feel? I feel sorry for them, but I still like the place where God called me. And I still like my fellow Koreans.

51

AN UNKNOWN MISSIONARY

One day in 1976, after returning to college from my military service, a friend suggested I visit a mission training center in Seoul, a place where missionaries were praying together and training for team ministry in the future.

This was during the early stages of missions in Korea, when only a few churches mentioned missions. I did not know who missionaries were or what they did. I was interested in learning English and finally went there with my friend.

To my surprise, the team leader was not a foreign missionary but a graduate student in seminary. He was thin, with high cheekbones and an exotic look. He already spoke fluent English and had great insight into history. I began to open my heart to missions as I watched his gentle manner, kindness, love and strong leadership.

I was greatly challenged and strongly felt that I must do my part in missions. This was the beginning of my mission commitment. After the seminary student leader graduated, he left us for missionary work as he had dreamed. I heard he had wanted to go to Nigeria but was not admitted into that country, so he was serving in another country in Africa.

Some of us who regularly attended those meetings have gone out as missionaries as well. This man might not remember me because I was neither active nor vocal in the meetings. If he knew I was serving in West Africa as a missionary, he would be quite surprised. When he was challenging us, not many churches and people even knew about the meetings.

I don't know why I miss him now. He seemed born to be a missionary and has devoted his life to service without making a name for himself in missions. He has not taken a furlough nor been a speaker at a missions conference nor written for a mission magazine even though he has been on the field for more than ten years now. He could be a well-known missionary as well as a main speaker, but instead is quietly doing evangelism among the Africans. He might hear about what I am doing and how I am bragging about my small ministry and fruit as if I am the only one doing great missionary work in Africa.

I try to restrain myself from contributing articles to Christian magazines, but I am not mature enough to repress either my hidden heroism or the putting on of airs about my achievements. What is he doing now? Does he have enough supporters for his ministry because he has been unknown to churches and people? What would he think about my writing?

We need more genuine missionaries like that man from Korea. Not only myself, but other workers as well have labored to learn a new culture and language. I could clearly see tremendous needs in Africa. When my Korean supporting churches heard what our team had done here – building a clinic, a training center, and a library, they were delighted and encouraging.

Actually, it is amazing that his sending church still supports him even though he never comes home from the field. There are churches that cut off support unexpectedly because there has been no communication from the missionary on the field, when what has happened is that the missionary's report has mistakenly been sent to a wrong address.

I know that by putting my stories into print I have no possibility of being an unknown missionary. Nevertheless, I am very proud of this man I've written about because I feel that there is at least one genuine missionary like him among my Korean predecessors in missions.

52

MANGO MAYHEM (CONCLUDED)

Remember my fine ripening crop of mangos from the first chapter? Two weeks before harvest time, we found ourselves returning to Korea to take up leadership of the new WEC Sending Base there. Half a month more, that's all it would have taken. Yet, I would have to leave my mangos behind. As the day of departure edged closer and closer, I would roam around the trees searching, on the slightest chance that one of the mangos may have miraculously ripened early.

As we prepared to leave Africa, my wife and I were perusing our belongings, trying to decide what to take with us and what to leave. At the end of the day, the only things we decided to take to Korea were our children (after much consideration), and some clothes (the ones that hadn't turned an odd yellowish color from the blistering sun). Our one electronic device that we had cherished and treasured, our old camera, didn't even seem worth taking home so we gave it away. The only thing I actually did want to take with all my heart was impossible to bring along. We couldn't delay our departure date over some fruit, nor could we take unripe mangos with us into Korea.

The evening before we left for Korea, I sat under a mango tree watching the fiery hot sun finally disappear behind the horizon. I closed my eyes and heavy tears began to fall. I felt an ache in my heart as questions began to race through my head. "Throughout my years here, what have I given to this country, to these people? Have I done my job? Have I done all that I could have done? Was it nearly enough? What will these people do now? How far will they go?" I looked up at the leaves of the mango tree and felt a wave of embarrassment. I had spent so much time and effort obsessing about these trees that my first thought when I was asked to go to Korea was, "What about my mangos?"

Despite all the sweat and tears that I had shed for these people, at that life changing moment I had stood there, not as a missionary under the calling of God, but rather as a hopeless mango farmer reluctant to leave his precious crops. Why had I become like this? I felt pathetic and shameful. As I dusted myself off and got up to go inside, it felt as though the mangos were staring down at me saying, "There goes that pitiful missionary ..." The following day, my family left Africa. We said our tearful goodbyes to our dear local friends and our fellow missionaries, to our house, to the blistering heat, and to our mangos.

A couple of chaotic weeks adjusting to the new environment and settling down in Korea passed and we made our first phone call to Africa. After a few minutes of greetings, I immediately asked about the mangos. "How big are they? How many mangos are there? How did you harvest them?" The questions were endless, and with no mercy Francis, the compound manager, went on and on about how the trees were dripping with mangos, how incredibly sweet they were, how there were enough mangos for everyone in the compound, for the entire village, and even for all our fellow missionaries. Throughout the years, the mango trees have continued to yield hundreds of mangos, enough to fill the stomachs of many hungry people, all except for the one hungry missionary who planted them – me. After spending hours and hours, drenching all my clothes with sweat, covering myself in dirt, planting and watering those trees, I have not been able to taste one fruit of the harvest.

God spoke to me with a gentle voice, reminding me, "This is your life, the life of a missionary. Just as a tired farmer plows through dry land and plants his seeds on a hot summer day, some missionaries travel to parched mission fields to plant these seeds of life in the hearts of the people. Many of these missionaries never get to see the products of their hard work. Some missionaries are called to the mission fields to continue the work and water the seeds that previous missionaries have planted. These missionaries spend their whole life walking through the wide fields, simply watering and nurturing these seeds. Just as Paul planted the seeds and Apollos watered them, some lead the way, shedding tears as they fervently plant seeds of the gospel while some follow, diligently watering them so that the seeds may bloom and bear fruit. Finally, some tread the fields harvesting the fruit of the grounds that were soaked with another's tears as he spread the gospel and another's sweat as she lovingly cared for the new blossoming trees."

Just as I have planted my seeds in Africa, others will be called to finish the work and harvest the mangos. They will harvest new African missionaries that have budded from my sweat and tears, and send them out to do their own planting. We are like mango farmers, called to our Father's fields at a time He assigns to devote our lives to doing the specific work that He calls us to do, whether it be planting, watering, or harvesting the mangos. This indeed, is the life and the joy of being a missionary: being able to plant something true and whole that others may come and benefit from, allowing them to effectively continue God's work, bringing delight and glory to Him.

I had to give up my obsession with the mangos of Africa. The time had come for me to obsess about mangos elsewhere and plant new seeds wherever God called me. I will run to wherever He sends me to plant the seeds because this, I know now, is my job. I have one hundred percent faith God will send others to follow and finish the job for me, so that in the end we may all enjoy God's bountiful harvest together.

Lightning Source UK Ltd.
Milton Keynes UK
14 April 2010

152768UK00001B/7/P